"Dear Sir,

Upon my mother's advice, I am writing this letter to you appealing for help.

We've desperately appealed to the council to get us out of our unfit house, but to no avail. I have written to the housing manager more than a dozen times and I have had more than a dozen letters from him all saying roughly the same thing. I have letters from my doctor—I have tried new towns without success. The house is so damp our clothes go mouldy; we have had to buy electric blankets for the beds because they get so damp. We cannot have open fires because the house is unsafe. I have to work at factories in the evenings to scrape the money together for the heating of this house. I see my husband for ten minutes each evening and half an hour in the mornings each and every day. When we do see each other we argue. We have bought new furniture to try and make a home for ourselves, but it has all gone mildew.

My eldest son suffers with severe colds, my youngest son has a blood disease. I don't know if he will live or die. My children have to play in the streets because we are infested with rats from the stables next door. The condensation from my kitchen goes into the bathroom and peels off the paintwork, the walls are going black because of it, and I can't bring myself to wash the walls down again because it takes too long and I can't stand it any longer. All I want to do is cry. I can't go on much longer. I think I am going insane. All I want is a nice home, a home to be proud of. A home to fetch my children up in without being ashamed of what they may think. My eldest son's schoolfriends laugh at him and call him names because of where we live. Nobody will come home with him because it looks so shabby. They call him a gypsy because of where he lives. He comes home crying because they call his house a wooden shack. It's unbelievable but it's true. I see my son break his heart because he too is ashamed of the house we live in. We are not gypsies, we never have been, we have always been brought up in respectable homes. Inside our house is clean and tidy, but outside it is a shambles. We have no friends because we are ashamed to let anyone know where we live. My whole family suffers because of this house, mentally and physically. My husband's morale has broken down into nothing. My children's pride is hurt–and me, I just watch on, see them suffer, and I suffer with them because I know what goes on in their minds.

They hate coming home, because of what it is, and I hate the thought of them having to come home to this. There is nothing to live for because there is no happiness in our lives, nothing to laugh about, just work, work, work, to stay warm and eat as cheaply as we can. In my mind, I wish someone would murder us in our sleep, because I haven't the guts to commit suicide. I have often thought about it. There are easy ways of killing oneself but I can't do it. I know my children would be better off if I was to die, and my husband would have no worries then, but I can't do it. I just can't. Please help us, please, you are our last hope now, and if nothing comes of this I shall die, not by committing suicide but of shame and loss of all hope of a new home.

Yours faithfully,"

I KNOW IT WAS THE PLACE'S FAULT

DES WILSON

. . . I'll not return;
There's nothing there I haven't had to learn,
And I've learned nothing that I'd care to teach –
Except that I know it was the place's fault.

Philip Hobsbaum
"The Place's Fault"

OLIPHANTS

OLIPHANTS
BLUNDELL HOUSE
GOODWOOD ROAD
LONDON S.E.14

ISBN 0 551 00791 5

Printed Offset Litho in Great Britain by Cox & Wyman Ltd, London, Fakenham and Reading

Typesetting by Print Origination, Liverpool

Contents

AUTHOR'S NOTE

In writing this book I've drawn shamelessly on my own original material - articles written for "The Guardian", reports edited or written for SHELTER, and speeches made at conferences or SHELTER rallies.

I would like to thank . . .

*"The Guardian," for allowing me to draw on the columns I wrote for it, and indeed for encouraging me to write them in the first place.

*Philip Hobsbaum, who allowed me to draw my title from his poem "The Place's Fault", published together with other poems by Macmillan.

*The SHELTER Team, for all their encouragement and help - especially my secretary, Barbara Evans, who typed the manuscript; my assistant, Helene Middleweek, who helped with the research; Ian Mattingley, who designed the jacket; and Nick Hedges, who took most of the photographs.

*You, my reader, . . . for being my reader! I trust your compassion for the homeless will extend also to my lack of literary merit.

Finally, I want to say thank-you to all of the people all over Britain who have helped me to help the homeless in my time as Director of SHELTER.

Des Wilson
September, 1970

PROLOGUE

When B.B.C. T.V. screened Jeremy Sandford's drama-cum-documentary about a homeless family, "Cathy Come Home", on November 15, 1966, it created a public uproar. While the Minister of Housing, Anthony Greenwood, ordered officials to a private screening, the Leader of Birmingham City Council, Alderman Frank Griffin, said of the cast: "They are just puppets strutting across the screen, poisoning the minds of the people watching." The play was repeated twice on British television and shown and acclaimed all over the world. The B.B.C. won awards. Carol White, the actress who played Cathy, went to Hollywood, but . . .

WHATEVER HAPPENED TO CATHY?

For over an hour Britain was captured by Cathy—Cathy hitch-hiking to London, Cathy meeting and marrying a delivery driver, Cathy having a baby, Cathy's husband getting badly hurt jumping from his skidding lorry, Cathy's family moving to a squalid tenement, then a derelict caravan site, then a hostel for the homeless, then Cathy being evicted, and finally Cathy's family breaking up.

Jeremy Sandford wrote:

> **"And then Cathy was filled with some fund of energy that she hadn't known about. She was like an animal now, as she fought to keep her children. And they overpowered Cathy and held her down and the children were carried off. Cathy screamed, yelled and then her sobs subsided. She was left, moaning to herself.**
>
> **"A passer-by asked Cathy was she all right and she said she was all right.**
>
> **"She rose from the seat and went to the 'All-Nite T Bar' and spent her last fourpence on a cup of tea.**
>
> **"She had one penny left."**

Britain was indignant. If this gaping hole in the Welfare State couldn't be kept decently under the carpet then someone somewhere had to be blamed!

So the Labour Party blamed among other things the thirteen years of Conservative administration, and the Conservatives blamed - among others - Socialist-controlled councils. The political-left blamed the capitalist system for obtaining its profits by exploiting scarcity, and the political-right blamed socialism for restricting provision with planning and rent controls. Newspapers analysed and demanded and you could hardly move across London for taxi-loads of articulate "spokesmen" racing to television studios to explain on "24 Hours" or "News at Ten" exactly what happened, and how, and why.

Indeed, when Britain gets cross about something, so comprehensive is the media coverage, and so intense the heat engendered, that the uproar created is sometimes self-defeating. For what's "topical" today can be "old hat" tomorrow, and the public are apt to assume that the problem ends at the same time as the headlines. Sometimes the victims of a problem are left wondering whether the media did anything for them, or whether in some way they've been temporary servants of the media.

What, for instance, happened to Cathy? The real Cathy? Where did she go? Where is she now?

My guess is that, for all the hullabaloo, Cathy is still homeless.

Because, for all the hullabaloo, the emergency end of Britain's housing problem is worse.

In 1966, for instance, there were 12,411 people in hostels for the homeless. In 1969 there were 18,849.

Greater numbers of casualties can be blamed on greater scarcity—in 1966 there were, for instance, 150,000 families on local authority waiting lists in London. In 1969 there were over 190,000.

It's possible Cathy never saw her husband, Reg, and three children, Sean, Stevie, and Melane again.

It's possible the children are among the 7,000 odd, who will tonight toss and turn in the beds of our childrens' homes–what we call " in care" - for one reason only - their family haven't a decent home. The bewildered children of beaten parents.

Alternatively, the family might be back together again, back in a hostel for the homeless - what the authorities call Part III Accomodation. Probably locked in at 10 p.m. and locked out at 10 the following morning. Sharing a dormitory with others. The place deliberately kept unsatisfactory to "encourage them to find something better". Housing's skid-row.

Most probably Cathy and Reg and the children did come back together again, but, now struggle to survive as a family in an overcrowded and squalid slum. Homeless by any civilized definition. Homeless along with at least a million other men, women, and children.

For them, all signposts point to the twilight zones, the ring of inner boroughs in London where more than half of Britain's multi-occupied houses are to be found–in North Kensington, Paddington, Willesden, Hammersmith, Islington, Stepney, Hackney, and others; the rings of decaying, overcrowded houses in Birmingham and Liverpool; the rings of tall, grey, gloomy tenements in Edinburgh and Glasgow.

If that's where Cathy is, she could be paying anything between £2 in Scotland and £6 in London for an inadequately furnished room, or room and a kitchen. No bath - probably no hot water. Cold water from a tap on another landing. Lavatory (if working) shared with other families. Conceivably plagued by beetles, cockroaches, mice, and even rats. No real security of tenure - not even since the Rent Act if she's in a furnished room–and no privacy.

Cathy, still in her twenties, will already look old. She'll be apathetic and lethargic. Her skin will be unhealthy and her nerves will be raw with the strain of looking after children in one damp, dark, overcrowded room. Most of the time she'll be afraid to let them play out in the streets where they could be mowed down by a passing car or picked up by a stranger too far away, four floors below, for a cry of panic to be heard.

She'll be rowing with too many neighbours over too few facilities.

She'll be living in fear - afraid of eviction and afraid of destruction (the risk of an unexpected blaze caused by an upturned paraffin heater is always there).

She'll be needing her husband's help with the children when he gets home from work, but will be half afraid that another night of the tension caused by overcrowding will lead him to walk out and spend their precious money on drink, or even go for good.

For he, too, is probably tired and ill. Can't pull his weight at work because he doesn't get proper sleep. The faster he runs, whether in the race for housing or work, the slower he seems to go.

And the children . . . still too young to go to school, they will play in that room all day, except when Cathy can sit down in the street to watch them play in gutters that could spread disease or on abandoned cars littered with broken glass. Sometimes at night, jumbled two or three to a bed, they might even be awake to see Cathy make love to her husband–whenever they can pick up the strands of affection or the strength to try.

Chances are that's what happened to Cathy. If she came home, it was home to hell!

Tragic. But the real tragedy is that her story is in no way exceptional. The desperate faces of families trekking to the SHELTER Housing Aid Centre in London testify to that. So do the desperate letters and phone calls to SHELTER headquarters. But no need to take my word–the hideously–squalid houses and neglected streets are there to be seen, and the families there to talk for themselves.

"The Times" sent writer Adam Fergusson to see for

himself. He wrote:

> **"That it is possible in Britain today to be literally homeless, and that thousands of families are as destitute and blameless as though an earthquake had hit them, is the plain truth . . . many thousands of displaced families are playing a ghastly game of musical chairs, looking not only for new houses but for hovels which cannot be dignified with the name of home . . . There is large scale human agony among the casualties of the system, with whom the statutory bodies are not equipped to cope."**

It's not for nothing that the word "problem" is always attached to housing. Indeed any word association beginning with *housing* would inevitably end up with *scandal*. The facts and figures of the housing problem both before and after Cathy, and the stories of human need that lie behind them, reflect a staggering national social failure.

As a nation, we are nearly always at the foot of the Western European league tables for expenditure on housing. We've never given housing the priority it deserves, and Cathy made no difference to that. As individuals, we never wanted to hear the cries for help before Cathy, and even now we prefer to hear the strident voice of prejudice against the homeless than to accept the sacrifices we must make to save them.

The opportunity has been there in the 25 years of increasing affluence since the Second World War to attack and solve Britain's housing problem. That opportunity was never taken. Not that we did nothing. Just that we settled for inadequacy–inadequate priority, and inadequate performance!

And so in 1970 we find well over a million human beings in Britain living in fear, jumbled on top of one another, strained and tense, humiliated by the lack of privacy and stripped of dignity by lack of ordinary facilities, threatened with ill-health by dampness and infestation that spread disease, sometimes in physical danger because their house is so unfit, and sometimes literally tossed into the streets, to be taken into hostels that can vary from just passable to punitive.

The homeless work, but they can't earn enough. And even if they could, the homes aren't there to be paid for. They've tried to help themselves, but there's nothing they can do.

One of the things about Cathy that shocked was that she was at *our* mercy—at the mercy of *our* authorities and institutions, *our* policies and *our* priorities. *And she was getting no mercy*. After all, the only mercy you can give a homeless family is a home.

Cathy, the work of SHELTER over the past four years, and this book, all appeal before the court of public opinion for justice. They ask you to find the homeless are, as "The Times" writer put it, "as destitute and blameless as though an earthquake had hit them". They ask you to find the housing problem an intolerable scandal, and the society that allowed it to happen guilty of apathy and neglect, hypocrisy and greed. But, in hope, they ask you not to pass sentence on others, but rather to take positive action yourself. You *can* help the homeless. And you *can* influence others to mobilize the resources of manpower and money needed to solve the problems. In his book, "To Seek a Newer World", Bobby Kennedy wrote:

> **' Each time a man stands up for an ideal, or acts to improve the lot of others, or strikes out against injustice, he sends forth a ripple of hope, and crossing each other from a million different centres of energy and daring, those ripples build up a current that can sweep down the mightiest walls of oppression and resistence."**

You and I, as individuals, may be the ripples. But brought together, as members of political parties, in voluntary organisations with a common cause, mixing compassion with determination and asking for no more than elementary justice–that every family in our land should have a chance of a decent home–we can build the currents that will sweep down the walls of slumdom in Britain and liberate our homeless.

It is not only the fate of the needy that is at stake, for when generations to come pass their verdict on Britain in the 1970s, and ask, "Whatever happened to Cathy?", the answer will also tell them, in terms of priorities and values, exactly what happened to us.

ONE THE HOMELESS

"Let the bleedin' bastards who smoke, drink and gamble keep their own vile small bastards–not beg from the poor."

Anonymous letter to Des Wilson.

"Though all society is founded on intolerance, all improvement is founded on tolerance."

George Bernard Shaw

WHO ARE THE HOMELESS?

Britain's housing crisis is a major social and economic one, central to the well-being of our society. Such is its size and scope that any family handicapped by low income or any other physical or social obstacle is highly vulnerable. Indeed, housing is not just a problem in itself, but creates and intensifies the variety of other problems that contribute to social malaise.

SHELTER's 1969 "Face the Facts" campaign to get a sensible definition of the homeless was not, then, a play on words, but a most serious attempt to get the realities and dimensions of the problem better known, and consequently to get it more effectively tackled.

Despite the impact of "Cathy Come Home", and the sustained SHELTER publicity campaign, the popular view of the homeless in 1969 fell somewhere between heavy-breeding, heavy-drinking, heavy-gambling, unemployed layabouts and smelly, meths-drinking tramps.

There was little acceptance of the truth, namely that the homeless could be ordinary people, young people, even intelligent and hard-working people, all of them the losers in a highly competitive situation.

As John Greve has said in his Report on "London's Homeless" in the early 1960s:

> **"When the homeless become a topic for public discussion, accusation and counter-accusation, there is debate and speculation as to whether the homeless are 'feckless ne'er do wells' or 'ordinary decent Londoners'. There are echoes here of the Victorian insistence upon the distinction between 'deserving' and 'undeserving' poor. The research team found that the homeless were more likely to be decent than ne'er do well, but, in any case, there is little point–or humanity–in attempting to separate the victimised from the feckless and unvirtuous if the object is to help one but not the others."**

The trouble is that the word "homeless" has been officially linked with the word "welfare". Not only has the official number of homeless been falsified by definition, or lack of it, but the character of the homeless has also been falsified, and the authorities are able to infer that the homeless form a small group that would inevitably end up in the cesspool of any society.

The first aim, then, of a redefinition linking homelessness to housing need is a change of attitude, so that it can no longer be argued that the homeless are a feckless minority, and no longer automatically possible to reflect on their character, dragging in past records that are often irrelevant. No longer would the homeless be regarded as subjects for punitive and disciplinary action.

And so the aim of the "Face the Facts" campaign was to relate homelessness to housing scarcity, and not to welfare, (in its administrative sense) and get full recognition of the scale of the problem.

On April 29, 1969, the Minister of State for Health and Social Security, David Ennals, said of the homeless:

> **"There has been a great deal of exaggeration of the size of this problem and the numbers involved. I have even seen references to '3 million homeless'. This is really nonsense. In England and Wales there are 3,594 families living in temporary accommodation–a total of 18,689 men, women, and children.**

Mr. Ennals went on to say:

> **"I am speaking of truly homeless people those who have come to welfare departments for shelter in temporary accomodation."**

On January 16 of the same year, the Social Works Services Group of the Scottish Home and Health Department wrote, in answer to an enquiry from SHELTER to say that: "101 men, women, and children are homeless in Scotland."

To be fair to Mr. Ennals, he did not devise the definition. If he is to be condemned it is because he chose to defend it. But there can be little sympathy for the three Ministries–Health and Social Security, Housing and the Home Office–that perpetuate it.

There was a time when I brought gales of laughter from audiences by pointing out that when Ministers were asked why the number of homeless had increased, they replied that it could be because there was an increase in the number of hostels. If you took this to its logical conclusion, you could rid yourself of the problem overnight simply by closing down the hostels. There would then be, by definition, no homeless. This is something I don't joke about any more, for it's exactly what has happened in Birmingham and Newcastle, where the hostels were closed down and the homeless diverted to empty property in slum clearance areas on a "temporary basis". This policy is not in itself a bad one, but it does underline the absurdity of the official explanation, for both cities now claim with pride that they have "no homeless".

Too many officials think, talk and–what is worse–act in terms of administrative definitions. They live in an officially-defined fantasy world.

Excluded from the homeless, by most official definitions are:

1. Families "on the streets"–sleeping in an abandoned car, or in the open. (This again shows the absurdity of the official definition; having lost the four walls and a roof, the family have to regain them–"in temporary accommodation"–before they are homeless!)
2. Families living in squalor
3. Families hopelessly overcrowded
4. Families split up (including those with children "in care")
5. Families taken in under stress by in-laws or friends
6. Families in physical danger because of the unfitness of their property
7. Families lacking many or all of the essential facilities, toilets, hot water, etc.

All of the above families are *not* homeless in the eyes of most authorities.

Nobody would deny that *some* of the emergency homeless to be found in hostels confront the authorities with a variety of welfare problems. But not only does the stamp "welfare" attach itself to all of the homeless, whether they are welfare problems or not, it's misleading in two ways:

Firstly, it infers that the families do get welfare assistance, when often they don't, for many welfare authorities are more concerned with moving on the homeless than providing the help required.

Secondly, the welfare assistance often comes too late, in the sense that any welfare need that existed was there earlier, and had it been provided, the families concerned might not have needed shelter in temporary accommodation, in the first place.

My view is that public attitudes to the homeless are conditioned by the image of them projected by the authorities, and this lies behind our failure to give housing the priority it deserves. Priorities tend to be defined by what is known about the extent of the need, by the urgency of the need, and by the effect of the need on society as a whole. Partly because the homeless and the poor tend to be isolated from the majority physically and socially, the extent and the effect of their problems are not generally known.

A small and powerless group such as the 18,849 officially homeless are hardly likely to command priority over the many other demands on the nation's resources. But if the homeless can be seen for who they are, and how many there are, numbering hundreds of thousands instead of hundreds, we might hope for better. As the "Face the Facts" Report said:

> **"A policy of facing the facts may hurt our pride, but it is essentially a constructive one. When attitudes are changed, and the housing problem is given priority relative to its urgency, and relative to its social and economic ill-effects on society as a whole, we will be creating the real possibility of realistic and sensible policies."**

Who, then, are the homeless?

My definition, and the SHELTER definition, is based, firstly, on a faith in family life as the central part of the social fabric of our society, and secondly on the belief that just as food and clothing are *the* basic necessities in the life of the individual, so is a home *the* basic necessity in the life of a family.

There are times when a family might be best to break-up, but if we are to protect the institution then any break-up must be by choice, and not by force. Thus, when I talk about the homeless, I am referring to any family that is either split up because its home is too small, or living in housing conditions so unfit or overcrowded that it cannot lead a civilized family life.

A home should meet two criteria:

Firstly, it should be a place where individuals and families can be themselves for better or for worse, can obtain peace and security, and can thrive both mentally and physically unfettered by the prejudices and the pressures of the society that surrounds it. Whether quiet or noisy, clean or dirty, social or anti–social, there should be a place where everyone is, in almost every respect, answerable only to himself and his family. To this extent, I go along with the old saying: "An Englishman's home is his castle."

Secondly, the home must be an effective base for daily life. We are participating in the most highly pressurized and competitive society of all time, and to survive we need rest and relaxation and we need mental and physical stamina.

SHELTER claimed in 1969 that there could be as many as a million men, women, and children going without such a home. It's not SHELTER's fault that better statistics aren't available. It's a disquieting thought that better statistics could show the problem to be much worse.

Let's look in the remainder of this chapter at homelessness as it exists in multiple-occupation, squalor, or hopelessly overcrowded conditions:

Multiple Occupation

The multi-occupied house is not by definition a slum, but often it is in reality. The Housing Act 1961 defined it as a "house which or part of which is let in lodgings or which is occupied by members of more than one family". In practice, a multi-occupied house is usually sizeable, and occupied by several families occupying separate rooms, but sharing common entrances, yards, halls and staircases, bathrooms, lavatories, and often water supply, kitchen and cooking facilities as well.

The multi-occupied house is mainly a creature of the city. In London, for instance, nearly 25% of households live in multi-occupied houses (635,000 households) and the highest numbers elsewhere are also to be found in major conurbations, like Merseyside and the West Midlands.

A Ministry of Housing official, who carried out a review of multiple-occupation in 1966, wrote in his report:

> **'For the majority although a multi-occupied house may provide reasonably adequate accommodation for the time being, it represents something less than what would be regarded as a satisfactory permanent home . . . a great deal of it is thoroughly bad . . . most local authorities have to cope with a hard core of extremely bad cases were the tenants were living in most squalid conditions . . . some of the properties we saw were extremely overcrowded . . . we have inspected many houses where the physical condition of property was shocking. We saw lavatories that were not working, ceilings that had partially collapsed, rooms that were so damp that mould collected after a day or two on clothes left in the wardrobe, drains that were blocked so that the areas and yards were flooded, rotten floorboards, stairs and other woodwork, windows without glass or which could not be opened, a house in which electricity and gas supplies for four or five families had been cut off, innumerable leaking roofs. In one house we saw the rain running down a central electric flex and dripping into a bucket below. In another we saw a large**

> **growth of orange dry rot fungus a foot or more long attached to the ceiling. In many of these houses, bathrooms, if they were usable at all, kitchens and lavatories were shared by far too many people . . . we were shown one house from which the council have removed three tons of accumulated refuse from the cellar . . ."**

Multiple-occupation leads to a fairly speedy fall in standards. Bad management and maintenance are prevalent. The Ministry of Housing official wrote:

> **"We very soon found that we had very little difficulty in walking down a street and picking out many of the houses in multiple-occupation by familiar signs. They can be distinguished by a need for repainting, by unkept front gardens, broken fences and gates, defective gutters and drains, rubbish and refuse left lying about and a general air of neglect and decrepitude. Backyards and gardens are the same. In almost all of the houses we visited they seemed to be used only as a rubbish dump or perhaps a space for drying clothes. Broken plaster, dampness, defective lavatories, cooking equipment and heating and light appliances were common. The arrangements for storing refuse were also very often inadequate with a result that dustbins were spilling over because there were not enough of them, or the rubbish was dumped in the back garden."**

A not un-typical multi-occupied family is the Harper family, who live on the top floor of a house in Wandsworth. He earns £16 a week flat rate as a foreman stone cleaner, but works up to 16 hours a day so that they can save the money for a better home. The lavatory they share with six other people is in the basement, so they keep a bucket in the corner for the children who are afraid to walk down the steep and rickety stairs at night. There is no bathroom, no hot water, and even the cold water is stored in containers on their floor, because the cold water tap is in a small and inadequate basin on the landing below. Every time they want hot water for anything it has to be boiled on the stove, taking time and money.

Rain comes through the ceiling, peeling off the wallpaper, and making the room so damp that there is steam and condensation from the gas fire. There are mice in the living room, and also maggots. The children have suffered from bronchitis and the little girl's mattress had mildew in it because of dampness when we called. All sleep in one bed, and the children in two cots. There is considerable fire risk because the house is rotten, and the people next door had an accident with an oil heater causing a fire not so long ago. This worries Mr. Harper a lot. To add insult to injury, a railway line is so close to the house that, when trains are passing, the place literally shakes and you can't hear anybody speak. The Harpers have been on the council waiting list for five years.

Squalor

The committee set up under Professor Barry Cullingworth to look at "Scotland's Older Houses" said:

> **"Even the Glaswegian who sees only the often imposing (yet, on closer inspection, often crumbling) front exterior seldom appreciates how revolting and inhumane are the conditions inside the closures on the common staircases, and in the back courts. And even if he does occasionally glimpse the physical squalor which is out of sight to the passer-by, he can have no conception of the extent of the problem."**

Tom MacMillan, M.P. for Glasgow Central, stood in the Gorbals and told a SHELTER researcher:

> **"Gastro-enteritis is rife here, we lost one kiddy's life though before the building was condemned. You should come in wet weather to see all the stagnant filth and stink. The water piles up so that you can't even get through the passage on wet days. Look at those kids playing with those flea-ridden things by that rotting green pool! There are mice on the ground floor and rats on the top floor. The houses over there are empty, nobody will take them and as soon as that happens the rats move in. The rats are everywhere in Glasgow. The gutters are missing and the damp has invaded all the buildings. The people themselves may not see the reason in the winter for the old men's chronic chest troubles, the kiddies' wheezing and coughing–the house they're living in is rotting with damp. The man in that house with the black damp patch on the outside wall contracted chronic bronchitis. I reported the damp to the factor responsible a dozen times. Now it has got so bad that in this shop here, two floors down, an electrical explosion took place. I reported it to the police and told the factor again. He said he came three times and could never get into the shop. So I sent the woman along to give the times that she would be in but still nothing was done. Through that and other things like it they condemned the block. Now can you tell me the difference between this block and all those over there?"**

The Connell family, when we found them, lived in two damp, hopelessly overcrowded, and mice-ridden rooms in a rotting house squeezed between a derelict ruin and another empty house in Holloway, London.

There was no bathroom, no hot water, no proper heating. But there was dampness, rotten woodwork, and cardboard to keep out the draught from broken windows.

James Connell, who worked at night, and tried to sleep while the children played around the room in the daytime, paid £3 a week rent out of his income of £21 as a railway worker for their one room, 10 feet by 10 feet, and a kitchen.

Not far way in Upper Holloway a Public Health Inspector told another family we came across, the Stewart family, that their bedroom had been condemned in 1936 because of dampness.

Thirty-three years later the Stewarts were living in it. Both their two little children were bronchial. There was woodworm in the floor, the stairs were shaky and unsafe, and the lavatory was in a recess of the tiny kitchen/scullery.

Shirley Stewart was expecting a baby, but the flat kept getting flooded, as water poured from blocked drains upstairs and down the back wall to the kitchen. She had to carry heavy buckets of water out and mop up, and blames this for the fact that she had a miscarriage.

He worked as a carpenter earning £15 a week, and Shirley earned £7.10.0d a week in a factory. Their rent was £3.10.0. a week. They had been on the council wainting list for three years, and on the Out-of-Town list for six years.

Two families whose father was working, paying rent for the privilege of living in squalor.

Two of Thousands.

One of the main problems is dampness. The intensity of the dampness varies enormously, but in the twilight zones it is possible to find whole streets with dampness stripping wallpaper from the walls, permeating clothing and bedding; damp hangs in the air until it seems to dominate the lives of the people who live there. The homeless never stop talking about dampness, worrying about dampness, trying to cope with dampness, and they never seem able to get anything done about it. In nearly every case history collected for SHELTER you will find an instance of dampness.

This in turn causes or aggravates health problems.

Then there is the problem of infestation. We were stunned at the time of our "Face the Facts" research to come across not just beetles, bugs, and mice, but cockroaches and rats.

There was the case of Mr. and Mrs. Duke who lived in Liverpool, paying £2.11.0 for the two rooms and a kitchen that housed them and their five children. Cockroaches were their worst problem. They were so bad that the whole family slept in one bedroom and their light was kept on throughout the night to scare the cockroaches away. But Mrs. Duke says that sometimes in the morning the living room carpet was black with cockroaches. She said she complained to the health authorities twice in six months but nothing was done.

The Mullory family in Manchester with seven children living in four rooms, were infested with mice, rats and cockroaches. The mice nibbled away at the bedding in the baby's pram, and Mrs. Mullory began to suffer with nerves, from her constant terror of having to face the rats when filling the baby's bottle in the middle of the night, and from her fright when she frequently found rats in the beds when she was making them.

One of the most unpleasant aspects of unfitness is the "accelerated variety" found in the slum clearance areas. The moment an area is designated for slum clearance, all investment in it ceases. Local services are reduced even by the local authority, and any private landlords involved cease any expenditure whatsoever. Families begin to move out and houses become deserted. But some families can find themselves living there for several years, and others who possibly moved in after Compulsory Purchase Orders were served have nothing better to go to. Empty houses are invaded by vandals, or tinkers, and gradually stripped of their contents, becoming glorified rubbish dumps. Rats are disturbed as the houses cave in, and they move into the occupied houses. The occupied houses become as insecure as the deserted ones, with lead piping being stolen and people often having to walk long distances to find a water tap or a lavatory that is still working.

Danger

Many people don't realise that the homeless often live in fear and danger of their lives.

This is no exaggeration and the fatalities are there to prove it.

London's Evening Standard reported on January 21, 1970:

> **"For three years George Lewis and his wife tried to find a new home for themselves and their growing family.**
>
> **"When their third baby was born last summer the whole family had to share one bedroom, 10 feet by 12 feet, in a tiny basement.**
>
> **"And today a coroner blamed the size of the flat for killing three children.**
>
> **"For packed into the bedroom were two beds, a cot, a settee, a dressing table, chairs, and a paraffin heater.**
>
> **"St. Pancras Coroner, Dr. Harold Price, said: 'If they had had enough accommodation this tragedy could well have been avoided.'**
>
> **"While Mrs. Lewis was making a feed for the youngest baby she smelt smoke and found the bedroom ablaze.**
>
> **"She tried to fight her way through dense smoke to reach the children but was beaten back.**
>
> **"Fireman later found the bodies of the children: Garfield 3, Sonia 20 months, and Carolyn 6 months, all dead from carbon monoxide poisoning.**
>
> **"Fire Prevention Officer, Kenneth Innes said the bedroom was crowded with furniture.**
>
> **"He added that the only available space for the paraffin heater was just a few feet away from the door.**

> **"He believed it could have been knocked over by a young child trying to get out of the room.**
> **"Dr. Price, recording a verdict of accidental death, said:**
> **"I am aware of the difficulties of getting suitable accomodation. They were all sleeping in this ten by twelve room which was completely inadequate.**
> **"In this case it was the question of the overcrowding of a room and the only place available for going in and out of the room was where the heater was placed.**
> **"He added: 'A toddler must have knocked down the heater. This can happen if they are left on their own for only a minute."**

Three children dead. Burnt to death.

Also dead are two-year-old Jean Simon, John Murray (eighteen months), and the triplets Peter, Paul and Patrick Braithwaite (aged three years). Jean was trapped in the attic bedroom of a three storey house occupied by 14 people. Cause of fire: a paraffin heater. The Braithwaite triplets were suffocated in a fifth-floor flat. Cause of fire: an oil heater. John was suffocated in his cot, when thick black smoke filled his room. Cause of fire: a smouldering electric fire. One could go on, listing tragedy after tragedy.

The incidence of injury, such as burning, among the lowest income families is said to be up to ten times that in upper income families.

Referring again to the never-published report of the Ministry of Housing official on multiple-occupation, he said this:

> **"We were told by Fire Officers that when smoke and fire appear to cut off the obvious means of escape through ground floor exits there seems to be a natural tendency for people to run upwards away from it and to become trapped in upper storeys if there is no adequate escape route. In the West Midlands**

particularly, but in otner areas as well, we saw numbers of houses in which the roofs were contructed round a central staircase well which was lit by a single skylight in the roof. It was explained to us that if a fire spread to this wall the glass skylight could be expected to break and produce an up-draught so the result could be virtually a furnace. "Where families are living on each floor or perhaps even in each room, in a house of this nature, the potential sources are multiplied accordingly. Many will be living in rooms that were designed as bedrooms and the small bedroom grate though adequate 60 or 70 years ago is insufficient to heat a living room satisfactorily, particularly for people coming from much warmer climates to face the British winter. There is a strong temptation to build much bigger fires than grates can safely accommodate and we saw a number of cases of the wooden surround and mantlepiece having been scorched and charred as a result. In addition, many tenants introduce supplementary forms of heating into the room–either portable electric heaters or oil stoves.– The danger of the former is in over-loading what may well be an antiquated wiring system–particularly when connected by extension sockets to a lighting circuit. The latter tend to be in danger of being knocked over, particularly in rooms overcrowded with furniture where there is an added risk from the storage of paraffin.

"The risks of using these appliances are intensified in the houses of immigrants from some parts of the world, who do not appear to be familiar with them or their dangers. Thus in a number of houses we have seen five gallon drums of paraffin standing within a few feet of a blazing fire. And two or three of these had a string of washing suspended from the

> **mantelpiece to dry and more than once we have seen, in addition, glass bottles of lighter fuel standing on top of the mantelpiece.**
>
> **"These conditions in large houses, accommodating anything up to half a dozen families with no means of escape from the top floor except down the main staircase are a Fire Officer's nightmare."**

Nor is fire the only danger. Tom McMillan, M.P. for Glasgow Central, speaking in the House of Commons on February 19, 1970 described how a wall and chimney of a tenement building in his constituency had crashed through the houses of 44 to 50 Fisher Street, Glasgow, imperilling the lives of forty-three people. He had reported the danger a week previously. He told the House:

> **"The frightening thing is the procedure which follows when somebody reports that a building is dangerous. The present procedure is that the factor, (Scottish equivalent of a housing manager), the landlord or agent is informed and then there is a waiting period, which might run into months. During this time a very dangerous situation can develop where lives are put at risk.**
>
> **"My constituents are forced to continue to live in these dreadful buildings during this period of terror. I have had occasion in my area, as its Member of Parliament and a former city councillor, to report a large number of buildings as dangerous. I should like to give the House some examples of my experience.**
>
> **"There was a case where a City Engineer's representative and I went to examine a toilet stock, a 60 to 70 foot high block of toilets added to a building, which I considered to be dangerous. The engineer's opinion was the same as mine but did not carry the same urgency. A few days later, about 3 o'clock in the morning, the stock collapsed and only by the grace of God no one was killed. If the collapse**

had taken place at any other time of day there would have been people using the toilets who possibly would have been killed, and children might have been playing in the back courtyard into which the stock collapsed.

"Another example occurred in the vicinity of the near-tragedy on 1st February. In this case the City Engineer's representative and I both agreed that the building was dangerous. The factor was informed and he agreed to spend about £1,500 to make the building safe. Weeks passed before, under pressure from the occupants, a safety barrier was placed around the defective wall. This barrier, however, quickly became ineffective because of vandalism and children's activities, and indeed the wall collapsed before any remedial work was done.

"I will give another example of what is happening at this moment. In a large tenement building there is a bulging wall which the factor has been asked to make safe. This man is one of the best factors in Glasgow, but nevertheless months have passed and, so far as I know, nothing has been done. One of my constituents has complained to me that she lives in the top flat of this tenement which is about 70 feet high and she finds that her doors jam and that cracks have appeared in her ceiling. She has become a very frightened woman.

"Last Sunday I visited the house almost next door to the collapse of Fisher Street. The movement in the building was such that the amount of wood cut from the bottom of doors to make them close left a two-inch gap. In fact, somebody who visited the property told me it was like walking on a listing ship. From top to bottom of the building a huge crack has appeared, which my constituents point out to me every time I visit the building. They have observed

that it is getting bigger."

There has been a lot of talk about violence in our society. There is not one street in London that, cross fingers, I would not fearlessly walk down in darkness. But there are millions of so-called homes that I would be afraid to live in, for fear of fire or even collapse. The existence of such dangerous conditions are a form of violence by society on its under-privileged.

Any family living in such conditions is irrefutably homeless.

Overcrowding

Overcrowding, more than any other aspect of homelessness, contributes to so many of our social problems. It is the cause of many families splitting up. It creates unbearable tensions because it gives people no opportunity for privacy when they need it most. It forces people to behave in front of one another in a way that reduces their dignity as human beings. It gives children no chance to grow up in normal circumstances, and creates neurosis, tiredness, and imposes an intolerable strain on the happiest of marriages.

Mr. and Mrs. Varley and their seven children were hopelessly overcrowded in a damp, rat-infested house in Salford. The lack of privacy and overcrowding was such that their fifteen-years-old daughter, who was in the A stream at a Grammar school, had to do her homework in the outside lavatory for peace. If one of the family wanted to wash, the rest had to leave the kitchen.

There was no bath, and so they boiled all their hot water on the stove and washed from the kitchen sink. Mr. Varley, an £18-a-week driver, and his wife, shared their bedroom with the four youngest children. All of the children suffered from bronchitis and were constantly ill throughout the winter.

This family's circumstances are in no way unusual.

TWO

"The problem is those without homes; and the problem is those living in slums; and it is the same problem of human misery."

Prime Minister Harold Wilson
Labour Party Conference, 1969

"There are millions of houses still decaying . . . 2 million slums, and 4 million in poor repair . . . perhaps a quarter of the people in this country today live in conditions like that. It is time to take the heartbreak out of housing."

Conservative Leader, Edward Heath,
Conservative Party Conference, 1969.

"Our society tolerates a million men, women, and children living in hostels for the homeless, or in rat-infested hovels, where a broken lavatory may be shared by 20 people, and four people sleep in one bed . . . decent people trying to bring up children in impossible conditions. They are the casualties of callousness amidst affluence, a rebuke to our sense of values, as once were the child labourers of the dark, satanic mills."

Liberal Leader, Jeremy Thorpe,
Liberal Party Assembly, 1969.

WHAT IS THE HOUSING PROBLEM?

The background to the problem of the homeless is poverty and a scarcity of housing.

In 1964-66 the Labour administration in a White Paper, "The Housing Programme for England and Wales 1965-70", showed that the housing problem had reached breathtaking magnitude, but although it caused a bit of a stir at the time, it failed to create anything like the scandal it justified. One can only assume that the problem had become beguilingly big, and a sense of fatalism prevailed, with the public assuming that "the housing problem has always been there, and always will."

Anyway, the White Paper said:

> **"In Great Britain some three million families still live either in slums, near slums, or in grossly overcrowded conditions."**

The White Paper said that we needed 3,700,000 houses immediately to replace slums, to overcome shortages, and to encourage mobility. Each year a further 180,000 would be needed. Thus, it said, the target of 500,000 houses a year by 1970 was modest in the light of the housing need.

The Scottish housing programme, issued at the same time, showed that nearly a third of the houses in Scotland were over 80 years old. Up to 500,000 new houses were needed to replace houses already identified as slums or incapable of improvement, and to meet existing shortages, keep up with the formation of new households, and reduce migration.

In 1967 a fresh housing survey carried out in England and Wales showed that the situation was even worse than the authorities thought. One in eight houses, 1.8 million in all, were "unfit for human habitation". About five and a half million people were living in them. Another 4.5 million houses (involving thirteen to fourteen million people) were below standard, and many would need to be demolished.

Thus, 40% of dwellings in England and Wales were either totally unfit or sub-standard, or lacking amenities.

It appeared from this that slums were forming at twice the speed they were being replaced, for in 1955 the local authorities had estimated the number of "unfit houses" at 853,000.

(Mark you, the statistics for the housing problem are so erratic and inconsistent, and predictions so unreliable, that even the deductions we make from the so-called facts must be made with the utmost caution.)

Nevertheless, it's clear our slum clearance programme had been totally inadequate, and our failure to look after existing property and improve it from time to time, was making obsolescence not just a permanent aspect of the housing problem, but one of increasing dominance.

Alongside the figures for unfitness, and lack of amenities, were the figures for overcrowding. The 1966 Sample Census indicated that at least 1.6 million people were overcrowded (that's to say, living at more than one and a half persons per room, including the kitchen), and near to 400,000 of them were extremely overcrowded.

The figures for unfit housing and overcrowding reflect two aspects of the housing problem. Not all of the others are so easily illustrated with statistics. But a particularly telling statistic is the one quoted in the opening chapter–7,000 children are separated from their families and "in care of the State" for no other reason than that their parents were homeless, or living in unsatisfactory housing conditions.

Many families figure in each of the statistics–the same family, for instance, could figure in the number living in houses ' unfit for human habitation", and also the number "extremely overcrowded". It's possible that some of their children even figure in the statistics for children "in care". I don't want to labour the point, but incredibly such a family would not be officially homeless.

THE HOUSING SURPLUS

To anyone who has a home and is not involved in providing homes for others, the housing problem could, I suppose, seem remarkably simple: just a matter of equating the number of families in the country with the number of homes.

Partly because they believe the majority will be foolish enough to fall for this, apologists for the housing authorities began to claim repeatedly in 1969 that within four years there would be a "housing surplus" in Britain–indeed, a surplus of one million houses over families.

The statistic may or may not be correct (I can think of at least three previous predictions that were proved unfounded), but in any event it is irrelevant to the housing problem.

The first point to make about the housing *problem* then, is that it is an entirely different thing from the housing *shortage*.

The shortage is merely an arithmetical exercise and involves totting up all the houses in the country as a whole, regardless of where families have to live, and inclusive of slums, overcrowded properties, and on-going obsolescence.

The housing problem can be broken down as follows:

1. **The houses must be in the right place.**

They must be where people can get work, and where there are sufficient recreational and social facilities for them to prosper physically and mentally. At the present time, many of our so-called "surplus houses" are in parts of the country where there is high unemployment, and the most desperate need inevitably reflects the economic success of the region where it is to be found. It's no coincidence that Britain's housing problem is at its worst in cities like:

***London,** centre of the country's biggest conurbation, where the number of families on local authorities' waiting lists has increased by 25% over the past four years to over 190,000, and where over 100,000 houses are unfit for human habitation.

***Glasgow** centre of the Clydeside conurbation, where over 50,000 families are on the council waiting list and thousands more just gave up, where 70,000 (a third) of its houses are unfit for human habitation, more than 70,000 households have no hot water tap, and over 180,000 people are overcrowded.

The Report "Scotland's Older Houses" said:

> *"We have seen conditions in Glasgow that can be described only as appalling. Families are condemned to live in atrocious conditions which could shock the national conscience–and we believe would do so if they were better known."*

***Birmingham**, capital of the West Midlands, where nearly 30,000 families are on the waiting list, and 6,500 families apply each year. Over 50,000 people are overcrowded, over 40,000 homes are unfit for human habitation, and nearly 60,000 households have no access to a hot water tap.

***Liverpool**, centre of the Merseyside conurbation, where more than 70,000 houses are unfit for human habitation, over 40,000 households have no hot water tap, and 35,000 people are overcrowded.

All of the above figures would be worse if one took into account the whole conurbation.

For instance, the south-east Lancashire conurbation, covering Manchester, Bolton, Bury, Rochdale, Oldham, Salford etc. includes 125,000 dwellings (one in seven) unfit for human habitation.

Either we have to be more effective in dispersing the industrial and recreational life of the nation, or we must boost the provision of homes in existing population centres. Either is an unenviable task, and this one aspect of the problem–getting the houses in the right place–is sufficient in itself to explode the myth of the "housing surplus".

2. Our housing must be of adequate standard

Again the "housing surplus" does not reflect the difference between houses (units of accommodation) and "homes"–good, decent places for families to live in. The squalor that remains is massive and inhuman. The "Face the Facts" Report showed that although there are 1.8 million houses unfit, the highest slum clearance figures achieved (in 1966) were 83,000 in one year. At that rate, it would take well over 20 years to clear the 1.8 million alone. At the current rate of house improvements (maximum 130,000 houses a year) it would take over 35 years to bring the 4.5 million dwellings requiring repair, or lacking one or more of the basic amenities, or both, up to standard. A surplus of houses is one thing; an adequate supply of occupiable houses another.

3. Our housing must be relevant to need, in terms of size.

For far too long we've been catering for the Sunday newspaper colour supplement version of the ideal family of the pill generation–mother, father, boy and girl–and the result is that not only has private enterprise failed to make provision for the larger family, or the single person, but so have local authorities. Any organisation dealing with the aged will tell you that catering for their housing needs is a nightmare. Often the only answer to the problems of a larger family is to split it up. All families split up, and all families overcrowded–even families packed into one room–are included in the so-called "housing surplus".

4. People must be able to afford to pay for their housing

All current trends in house prices and rents reflect the irresponsibility of predictions about our "housing surplus" creating a buyers' market. If we *are* about to enter a buyers' market, why can fewer people afford to pay market rents and market prices than ever before? Increases in building costs and the prohibitive cost of land, together with high interest for borrowing, have pushed up the prices of houses for sale. The same factors, linked with a growing determination by local authorities to "balance the books", have pushed up council house rents until the incredible situation has arisen where even subsidised housing is beyond the pocket of the ordinary wage earner. I will return to this question when I discuss poverty, but it is important to recognise that if a family can't afford a home, a home might just as well not be there, and if a family is in the home, but spending so much on rent that it cannot clothe, feed, or heat itself properly, it is, again by any civilized definition, still homeless.

5. Our housing programme must relate itself to tomorrow. That is to say it must take into account obsolescence, rising expectations in terms of standards, mobility, of the population, variable household sizes, change in birth rates, etc.

POVERTY

The "you've never had it so good" electoral strategy of the Conservatives at the beginning of the last decade, indiscriminate use of the words "affluent society", and superficial signs of universal prosperity–coloured television, and more cars per yard of road than any other country–have made poverty an apparently obsolete word in Britain.

Nothing could be further from the truth.

Britain has a "poverty line", in the sense that the minimum supplementary benefits are supposed to represent the minimum income required for civilized living in our society. Thus, anybody on the minimum supplementary benefits, or earning the equivalent, is living on the poverty line. Anybody with a lesser income lives below the poverty line.

In my view, the minimum supplementary benefits figure should itself be regarded as below the "poverty line", for it is far too low, particularly for families with children.

But, even so, the existing figures for poverty in Britain are staggering.

In his much respected book, "Poverty in Britain And The Reform of Social Security", A.B. Atkinson says:

> **"I estimate that between 4% and 9% of the population have incomes below the supplementary benefit scale. It seems likely that the figure is nearer the upper rather than the lower end of the range, which would mean that around 5 million fall below the level which the Government considers to be the national minimum."**

This would mean some two million households living below the poverty line in Britain, he argues.

That poverty exists on this scale in a nation of Britain's wealth is unacceptable.

What is even more unacceptable is that the largest single group among the poor or borderline poor are poor because they work for the remainder. They are in the public services. They work on buses and trains, they deliver the post and collect the dustbins, they sweep the streets and clean and repair the drains, they work in our hospitals and schools and serve a society that is too selfish to serve them.

The people in the service industries are a reflection on the exploitation of the less fortunate, or in the case of nurses and teachers, of the idealistic by the materialistic. Their existence on or near the poverty line reflects as badly on the trade unions as it does on salary-earning professionals, and particularly badly on the politicians who cater for the mass, at the expense of the minority. As a matter of expediency the minority are economically crushed.

And their relevance to the housing problem is obvious—they are its inevitable victims. Wherever there is scarcity of a basic necessity of life, there is intense competition, and exploitation. The inevitable losers in the competition are the poor, for the easiest to exploit are those who are being exploited already.

The poor can't afford to buy a house. (They can't even save the money for a deposit, let alone pay back their loan.) The poor can't afford the tiny number of privately-let flats that come on the market to rent, and no subsidy is available to help them. In the year 1970 it's also fair to say that the poor in many cases can't afford to rent a council flat.

Even the housing associations subsidised by SHELTER are struggling when it comes to helping the poorer families.

Let's just take one of the 2.7 million men earning under £17 a week in 1968—the one adult man in six receiving a poverty or near-poverty wage for a full week's work. Let's assume he wants a home for himself, his wife, and two children in London, where he has to live in order to get work (for the rest of the country all of the figures quoted will be lower, but so will the incomes). He has three choices:

1. **House Purchase**

An old house in London costs, on average £5,996 in 1970 and a new house, on average, £7,519. The average loan from a building society (and remember this is for the "average" person) is 66.4% on an old house and 62.7% on a new house. So he has to find £2,400 for a deposit. This is clearly ridiculous on his income. But nor is that all the money he will need. The building society will lend on average 2.7 times the purchaser's income.

His income, then, is capable of funding a mortgage of only about £2,400, or less than half the price of the house.

Even a man on an average wage, which in 1969 was £1,250, before deductions, wouldn't stand a chance.

On a poverty wage, even mortgage repayments on a 100% loan, if it were possible to get one, would be out of the question.

In other words, house purchase can be rejected as a possibility.

This was recognised in the 1965-70 White Paper, which said:

> **"It would be criminal at the present time not to allow for an even faster growth of building to let. Shortage falls heaviest on those least able to pay a high price for their homes. The families in the really bad housing conditions–in the slums, overcrowded, in multi-occupation–are in general, families who can only afford to rent, and who in most cases cannot afford to pay an economic rent . . . in particular, the conditions of housing in big cities makes a provision of a large pool of houses to let at rents below a profitable level an urgent social necessity . . . we are faced with an ever growing shortage of accommodation within the means of the poorer families: and the growth of owner-occupation can do very little to relieve it."**

2. **Council housing**

There are over 190,000 queuing up for a council house in London, at a time when council house building has fallen back. Thus the chances of a family getting a council house are practically nil.

But assuming our family is fortunate, and is offered a council house, the possibility is that the family won't be able to afford it.

The tendency has been to bring rents up, and to introduce rent rebate schemes allegedly to help the poorest families. But there is abundant evidence that many local authorities avoid rehousing the poorest families because they are regarded as too heavy a burden on rates.

Nor has the situation been helped by the fact that the Supplementary Benefits Commission has regarded some council rents as above an acceptable level, and refuses to pay the whole amount.

The above comments are most relevant to London, but as has been the case in the past with other aspects of the housing problem, are proving to be forerunners to similar problems in the provinces.

The main effect of the increasing financial difficulty of lower income families is that this, in turn, increases the pressure on council housing at a time when provision has fallen back. Thus rising rents and scarcity both stand in the way of a council house for the poor.

3. **Privately-rented housing.**

In the twilight zones, where our poor are forced to live, the private landlord is becoming extinct.

The political-right blames this on rent control, alleging that the landlord has been forced out of business. The facts do not bear this out, for even when the Conservatives were in power and lifting rent control, the private landlord was rapidly disappearing.

His place was being taken by the property speculator, who found that the incomes of the families seeking a home were a form of rent control in themselves. You can't get blood out of a stone. The families could just not afford an economic rent. So the speculators either gave up, or ruthlessly exploited the need of the families, by packing them into single rooms, at the highest rent they could afford, and making the maximum profit.

When the Labour administration came to power they introduced security of tenure, and the Rent Officer and the Rent Tribunal machinery. Now it was possible to appeal against your rent.

But one problem remained: no matter what way you looked at it, the families who needed to rent the multi-occupied rooms and flats in the twilight zones could not afford an economic rent. So either you encouraged the private landlord to remain, but the families who needed the homes to go, or you let the private landlord go, in order that the people who needed the homes could remain. Housing associations were seen as an alternative to the private landlord, and there is no question that they could let more cheaply because they had no profit motive. Even so, because housing subsidies are inadequate without a rent rebate scheme, it has been extremeley difficult to rehouse the poorest families.

Another consequence of the Labour administration's Rent Act is that, because its main provisions were not extended to furnished accommodation, unfurnished accommodation has virtually disappeared, and there is little more security of tenure than there was before the Rent Act. Many families are afraid to appeal against their rents, for fear of subsequent eviction, and many still pay exorbitant rents.

BRENT: 1970

Perhaps an understanding of the plight of the homeless in our twilight zones, the connection between poverty and housing need, results of neglect, and the effect of political bickering in housing, is best obtained from looking at one twilight zone and the council that controls it.

The London Borough of Brent was created by a merger of the predominently middle-class borough of Wembley, and the predominently working-class boroughs of Willesden and Kilburn. The working classes in the newly-established borough believe themselves to be oppressed by the middle-classes, pointing to the fact that they now come under a Conservative Council that established the headquarters for the Borough in Wembley, putting up the old Willesden Town Hall for sale, and moving all the social services to Wembley.

As one "Willesden born-and-bred" man put it to me:

"Now the poor must go cap in hand to the rich part of the Borough for the social services."

Whether this feeling of being dominated by the Wembley middle-class is justified or not, the flames of suspicion were fanned by the now-infamous Chalkhill affair.

When the present Council was elected in 1968 it inherited plans to rehouse families from slums on a pleasant estate at Chalkhill. The process of demolition in the Willesden slum clearance area, whence the families were to come, had begun in May 1969. The Conservative Council, who had never wanted Chalkhill to be a council estate in the first place, decided on rent levels between £6 and £11, exclusive of rates, central heating, costs, and things like the cost of a television aerial. This in itself immediately put the cost of homes in Chalkhill beyond the reach of most of the families in the slum houses, but, as if to make certain this was so, the Council decided not to extend its rent rebate scheme to the estate.

(All this in a Borough where the number of families on the Council waiting list had increased from 6,500 to 7,000 in a year, and where people were living in dreadful slums, badly overcrowded, and in prefabs!).

How then was the Council to fill the 3,000 homes that would eventually be available on Chalkhill?

Firstly, they made it clear that they would consider applications from people in the slum clearances, on the waiting list, and in existing council houses "provided they can afford the rent".

Because it was obvious that the majority would not be able to afford the rents, the Council added a fourth category: anyone living in Greater London for five years, provided the last year had been in Brent.

Then the situation became almost farcical: the Council began to advertise the flats! Thus families who might go without a desperately-needed home for years could, for the price of a local newspaper, see council flats, that they knew were standing empty, being advertised to anybody who could afford the rent.

The next unprecedented step was a decision by the Council that in order to ascertain that tenants could afford the high rents, it would expect two personal character references to come with any applications.

Defending this policy, the Chairman of the Housing Committee, Alderman Francis Pratt, said:

> **"We believe in the privacy of the tenant's private affairs. As long as the tenant is satisfied that he can meet the rent charged, we don't want to probe into his private affairs at all, and taking character references is one way of overcoming the problem . . . the rents on this estate are high and we don't want any tenants moving in and over-reaching their incomes to pay the rent."**

While this has gone on, the slum dwellers remain in slums, surrounded by boarded-up houses, in an area that is crumbling around them.

The Council's explanation for all this was that they had inherited a deficit on the housing revenue account of over one million pounds. If they introduced rent rebates, this would cost in the vicinity of £300,000 a year.

In other words, the Council had acknowledged the point made earlier in this book: the majority of working class families in an Inner London Borough cannot even afford the subsidised rent for a council house. This being the case, confronted with the choice between helping the families to pay the rent or balancing the books, the Council had chosen the latter.

I leave it to my reader to decide whether the Council had its priorities wrong. The most important lesson, from a national point of view, is that either the economics of housing or the subsidy system will need to be radically changed, or the spectacle of empty council houses and overcrowded slum families could become part of the national housing scene. Along with many other councils, the London Borough of Brent has also been responsible for cutting back its housing programme. The Minister of Housing reported to the House of Commons on November 25, 1969, that whereas the original programme was for 1,978 dwellings to be put to tender in 1969, his understanding was that there would only be 24—a shortfall of 1,954. In addition, the Council was putting to tender 387 dwellings deferred from previous years. At the same time, Phase IV of the slum clearance scheme at Stonebridge had been put back and would now not be completed for three years. He noted, too, that the London Borough of Brent had sold three sites to private developers on which 120 council houses could have been built.

Again the Council would argue, that, along with other councils all over the country, they were paying the price of national economic policies that had, in turn, led to interest rates at a record level, and rising costs across the board in the building industry.

But if one takes the effect of the Council's policy, and the accumulated sayings of Councillors and housing spokesmen, one has little difficulty in coming to the conclusion that this Borough is vulnerable to the charge that it is doing little to encourage poorer families to stay, and the effects of its policies are aimed at encouraging them to move, and there is a lack of compassion for the needy, and a lack of will to solve their problems.

For instance, the Council has been unco-operative when families offered to carry out improvements inside their properties, even properties owned by the Council, if the Council would make external repairs.

Another instance is the Council's neglect in the field of prosecution for harassment and illegal eviction. Even legal eviction is exceptionally high in the Borough.

But the Council can often be best assessed by its attitudes to the homeless, and here one must question

Brent's attitudes most closely.

In January, 1969, the Housing Manager of Brent wrote to SHELTER to say that if a family was completely homeless, their case would be considered by the Housing Department, and approved if the family had a long association with the Borough and their homelessness was not just due to their failure to pay rent "or some similar cause". No reference to investigation into why the family had been unable to pay its rent, why it was now in the Borough, if its association had not been that long, or what would be "some similar cause". He then went on to write about emergency accommodation, saying that it was usually provided "for the wife and young children". This is contrary to the Ministry circular asking that families should not be split up. He went on to say that "if the homelessness continues they are normally transferred to other hostels where they can live as a family unit."

It was also in 1969 that SHELTER's attention was first drawn to the Dartmouth Road Hostel, one of the worst in Britain. Conspicuous from the outside by its air of neglect, we found at one time twenty-two people of mixed sexes sleeping and living in one big room. Our researcher noted:

> **"The common parts, garden, yard, stairs and toilets are disgusting, there is broken glass and abandoned bedding, prams and decaying food lying around. This hostel is obviously totally inadequate. Talking to people at the Hostel, one concludes it is extremely difficult to be even informed of the existence of the hostel–all deterrent measures are used. On one occasion families were sitting for twelve hours in the Welfare Office, before the police were called to eject them. The police took the family to the hostel–much to the annoyance of the Welfare Department."**

On January 22, 1970, Pat Healy of "The Times" reported five homeless families, comprising five mothers and fifteen children, were sleeping "crammed together in a room 15 feet by 20 feet" in Willesden. This was the Dartmouth Road Hostel. Two families had been there for six weeks.

Her report said:

> **"Four of the families sleep in a part of the room about 15 feet square, partitioned off from the smaller, curtained section. Their beds are crammed together with no curtains to separate them. Some of the children share beds because there is no space for more beds. The room is the bedroom, sitting room, and playroom of the families and the lack of privacy induces frayed nerves among the tired mothers there. Husbands are not allowed to stay with their families."**

For some time we had been concerned about the insensitivity of the handling of families. If there's one thing that makes me extremely angry it is when a family is shunted from one place to another, without any reference being made to their destination. There's nothing that destroys the morale of a family more quickly than being told by one official to go and see another, only to arrive there and then be pushed on to another one, without ever seeming to come to the end of the road.

On several occasions the Welfare Department at Brent sent families direct to SHELTER's offices, although they well knew that SHELTER would only have to refer the family elsewhere. On no occasion did the Welfare Department bother to telephone first, and one can only assume that their only wish was to get the family out of their offices, regardless of the fruitless and disappointing journey the family would make, or the heartbreak and feeling of hopelessness that this action would create. The same practice was inflicted on the newly-set-up SHELTER Housing Aid Centre, and it was forced to send a letter to the Council on January 23, 1970, asking them not to do this.

Finally, SHELTER felt sufficiently concerned about the situation in Brent, and what could be learned from a national point of view, that it held a protest meeting there in February, 1970, and a letter was sent to the Council expressing concern at the lacking building programme, arguing that expenditure on rent rebates for the Chalkhill Estate were justified "if the flats are not to stand as a permanent monument to the lack of consideration of Brent Council for the needy and the homeless", expressing concern at the tardiness with which the allocation from the Urban Aid Scheme had been used, and at the way the Council dealt with homeless families.

Families were being evicted on overcrowding orders by the Council itself, and then the Council found itself unable to arrange alternative accommodation. The Council was urged to increase its stock of temporary accommodation, and asked to change its attitude to prosecuting landlords for illegal eviction. The Council's attitude, it was argued, was encouraging landlords to harassment and illegal eviction; it was urged that the Council should take stiffer measures and, as part of the welfare services, further information and advice on tenants' rights should be made available to families threatened with eviction.

In my view one of the things that has to be said about Brent, and other inner London Boroughs, is that their problems are quite beyond their own ability to cope.

It would seem to me that greater national responsibility must be taken for problems that may be local, in terms of their physical situation, but are national in the sense that the people in any locality do belong, and should be treated as though they belong, to one nation.

Hostels for the Homeless

Having referred to Dartmouth Road, I should comment briefly on other aspects of the problem of the emergency homeless–the families that really do need to be put up for the night because there is nowhere else for them to go.

Although I've argued in this book that the homeless extend far beyond families who end up in hostels, the latter group has reached a particularly low ebb, and in my view needs not merely rescue but a substantial boost back up the social ladder.

Yet our policies towards the emergency homeless vary enormously, being fair and humane in some parts of the country, and little advance on the workhouse in others.

One of the undoubted achievements of "Cathy Come Home" was to hurry the Ministries of Housing, Health and Social Security, and the Home Office into pushing out a circular to all local authorities calling for more humane treatment of the homeless who come to them for help, or temporary housing.

In particular, the Ministry asked that families should not be split up.

As can be seen from the information on Dartmouth Road above, not all local authorities have accepted the guidance inherent in that circular, but some have.

At the time of writing Professor John Greve is concluding a survey into the handling of London's homeless and a similar survey into the handling of the homeless in South Wales is also being completed. In view of the comprehensive nature of the reports they are expected to publish, I don't intend to devote as much time to the emergency homeless in this book as otherwise would be the case.

But there are a number of points one would wish to make:

Firstly, the number of families in welfare accommoda-tion does not give an accurate picture of the number without any home to go to. The number is restricted by the fact that such accommodation is limited. One Medical Officer of Health in London, answering a councillor's question, said recently that 10 families a week who were literally homeless were turned away because all the available welfare accommodation was full. Many other families find the conditions in welfare accommodation so appalling that they don't even apply, preferring some equally inadequate emergency accommodation elsewhere.

Secondly, many local authorities apply the rules and regulations with respect to the admission to welfare accommodation so rigidly, or apply their own interpretation of them so rigidly, that many families who are literally homeless are nevertheless not eligible for the accommodation.

One current practice in London, for instance, is to limit the accommodation to families who have been legally evicted; the consequences of this are reflected in the following case.

The W family were living in a relative's house on the understanding that they would vacate the house when the relative wanted it back. The father of the family began to make arrangements to buy a house and promised the relatives he would be out on an agreed date. But his negotiation for a mortgage fell through at the last minute, and when he had to leave the accommodation he and his family went to the welfare department.

The welfare oficer said he could not help the family because they were not officially homeless. They could only be regarded as officially homeless if they took legal action against the relative for harassment, in which case steps could be taken to reinstate the family so that it could be properly evicted, thus becoming officially homeless.

Naturally, the W family were not prepared to involve their relatives in such a legal dispute.

Eventually the family (mother, father, and three children) ended up sleeping in a car. The welfare department knew they were in the car, but still wouldn't regard them as homeless.

Cindy Barlow of SHELTER had a long dialogue with the Senior Welfare Officer, along the following lines:

Welfare Officer: We can't help this family. They are not homeless. They can only be regarded as homeless if they take the steps I have described.

Cindy Barlow: You know they are living in a car, and yet you won't call them homeless?

Welfare Officer; Well, they're not officially homeless.

Cindy Barlow: Don't you think your policy is unnecessarily rigid if it can't meet a case like this?

Welfare Officer: My authority is official Government policy.

Cindy Barlow: It can't be.

Welfare Officer: My authority is the 1948 National Assistance Act.

Cindy Barlow: Your authority is not the 1948 National Assistance Act.

Welfare Officer: I think I had better read the Act to you, as you clearly don't know what you are talking about.

Cindy Barlow: Don't bother reading the Act–I know what it says.

Welfare Officer: I'll read you the relevant sections as you don't know what you are talking about. It says the local authority must provide "temporary accommodation for persons who are in urgent need thereof, being need arising in certain circumstances which could not reasonably have been foreseen."

Cindy Barlow: And if you read to the end of the paragraph it says "or in such other circumstances as the authority may in any particular case determine". Am I correct?

Welfare Officer: Er . . . yes.

Cindy Barlow: And you agree that you do have a discretionary power which you are not prepared to use in respect of this family which you know is living in a car.

Welfare Officer: Yes.

Cindy Barlow: Why not?

Welfare Officer: Because they are not officially homeless.

Local authorities have taken a heavy hammering over recent years and tend to be highly sensitive to criticism. So let me acknowledge that there are many hard-working and humane people doing their best in very difficult circumstances for the homeless. But, having said this, it is necessary to say that all of our experience of dealing with the authorities suggests that there are still far too many people in local authorities whose attitude to the homeless is, at best, moralistic, and at worst, heartless.

Often the problems can be traced back beyond the officials to councillors themselves.

I couldn't begin to count the number of times I have practically had to bite my tongue off to avoid a row with some councillor who was making the most incredible generalisations about the homeless.

This problem of moralistic attitudes stretches beyond the emergency homeless to the allocation of council house tenancies.

The Cullingworth Committee, looking into allocation of council tenancies, was sufficiently concerned to say this:

> **"Part of our concern here stems from the feeling that there is a danger that applicants are graded according to an interpretation of their desert. This even extends, on occasions, to a rejection of some from the council house sector. We were surprised to find some housing authorities who took up a moralistic attitude towards applicants: the underlying philosophy seemed to be that council tenancies were to be given only to those who "deserved them", and**

that the most deserving should get the best houses. Thus unmarried mothers, co-habitees, dirty families, and transients tended to be grouped together as "undesirable". Moral rectitude, social conformity, clean living and a clean rent book on occasions seemed to be essential qualifications for eligibility–at least for new houses. Some attitudes may reflect public opinion . . . but this is a case where local authorities must lead public opinion."

In many cases reports are written where, in my view, they need not be.

A typical case was a family that applied to the SHELTER Housing Aid Centre to be moved to a northern town by its Out-of-London Scheme. The town in question requested a housing visitor's report from the local authority in London, and a recommendation as to their suitability for council housing.

The housing visitor reported that the family was considerably in arrears, with the implication that they were not reliable rent payers, and that the children were dirty, with the implication that they were not well looked after. They were not recommended. Their application for a council house was turned down, and soon after they became homeless, going into a hostel.

Yet two months after this report was written, a social worker connected with the welfare accommodation was asked to write another one, and this time the report stated that the accommodation the family had been living in was appalling, and that the family had withheld payment of the rent because of the bad living conditions, and because of harassment, and that when the family was taken to court for possession, a substantial sum was deducted from the arrears in view of the fact that the court considered that considerable blame lay with the landlady. None of this had got into the first report.

Then the report (the new one) went on to say:

> **"I would think that the bad living conditions there were certainly not the fault of the family, since their flat in the welfare accommodation is always clean, cosy and attractive. The husband is helpful in the home, making the beds and tidying the bedroom before leaving for work. The childrens' clothing is clean, and the children themselves chubby and well cared for. On arrival at the welfare accommodation, this family paid £1.10.0. above the rent required, and have remained in credit ever since. I would recommend this family as tenants."**

The disparity between the reports is a matter for concern in itself. But should either have been written? Here was a family that was prepared to lift itself up and move out of London, changing jobs, schools, and home, in order to create a better life for itself in a northern town. One housing visitor chose to write a derogatory report and the family were cheated of that chance. Why should either report have been necessary? It's tough on the second writer, who was so sympathetic to the family, but I am afraid that both reports laid equal emphasis on the "deserving" or "undeserving' nature of the family, when, in my view, neither should have been written.

The Price and the Prejudice

The problem of the homeless is not just a problem of discomfort. Society as a whole pays a heavy price for its existence.

Part of the price is economic (the cost to rid ourselves of the housing problem must be weighed against the cost of keeping it), part of it is the mental and physical health of the millions involved, part is the fact that it causes or intensifies nearly every one of our other social problems,. and part is the fact that it undermines the ideal of equality of opportunity for all.

As a society, we also pay the price for the prejudice

stirred up to obstruct rational thinking about the problems of the poor and the homeless–prejudices that ultimately will eat away at the soul of the society that tolerates them.

The following chapters look at the price we pay for the problem, and the prejudice that surrounds it.

Once, after a rotten day at school–
Sweat on my fingers, pages thumbed with smears,
Cane smashing down to make me keep them neat–
I blinked out to the sunlight and the heat
And stumbled up the hill, still swallowing tears.
A stone hissed past my ear–'Yah! gurt fat fool!'

Some urchins waited for me by my gate.
I shouted swear-words at them, walked away.
'Yeller', they yelled, ' 'e's yeller!' And they flung
Clods, stones, bricks–anything to make me run.
I ran, all right, up hill all scorching day.
With 'yeller' in my eyes. 'I'm not, I'm not!'

Another time, playing too near the shops–
Oddly, no doubt, I'm told I was quite odd,
Making, no doubt, a noise–a girl in slacks
Came out and told some kids 'Run round the back,
Bash in his back door, smash up his back yard,
And if he yells I'll go and fetch the cops.'

And what a rush I had to lock those doors
Before that rabble reached them! What desire
I've had these twenty years to lock away
That place where fingers pointed out my play,
Where even the grass was tangled with barbed wire,
Where through the streets I waged continual wars!

We left (it was a temporary halt)
The knots of ragged kids, the wired-off beach, behind the blinds. I'll not return;
There's nothing there I haven't had to learn,
And I've learned nothing that I'd care to teach–
Except that I know it was the place's fault.

Philip Hobsbaum

THREE

"At a time when Britain's most valuable natural resource is her people with their technical skills and mental ability, can she afford to have a high proportion of her people living in slum conditions, and have another generation of children brought up in slum conditions, inevitably at an enormous disadvantage to children from good homes. It is not too far fetched to imagine that the cost to the community of the slums and slum-life far outweigh what it would cost to solve the problem in the shortest possible time."

Winston S. Churchill, The Times,
October 20, 1969

THE PLACE'S FAULT

When Gordon Cherry, now deputy head of the Centre for Urban and Regional Studies at Birmingham, was working in Newcastle, he carried out a survey to compare the least overcrowded third of the city with the most overcrowded third. He established that compared with the least overcrowded third, notifications of t.b. were doubled in the most overcrowded third. Peri-natal death was 43% higher in the most overcrowded third. Venereal disease and offences against the person were both five times more prevalent and the figure for larceny only a little less. Persons on probation were seven times more numerous, juvenile delinquents three times more numerous, cases of child neglect five to six times greater, and mentally subnormal persons also three times more numerous.

Cherry concluded:

> **"The relationship is inescapable: overcrowding may be positively correlated with virtually all aspects of social malaise in Newcastle, often in a most marked fashion."**

I am not in the slightest doubt that comparisons between the most and least overcrowded districts of other cities would reveal similar social disparities.

The most serious aspect of the housing problem—more so, even, than the discomfort and misery that people endure—is the effect it has on the health and well-being of both the homeless and society as a whole.

We should attack the housing problem not as an end in itself, but as a beginning. The price we pay for slum-life is the undermining of family life, and the breeding of social problems. Such problems may not be solved when everybody is decently housed, but our chances of solving them will be greatly enhanced.

Effect on Health

The health risk is colossal. Dampness is the main threat, but sharing of the facilities and overcrowding are equally responsible for the spread of illness and disease.

In the winter both parents and children are nearly always cold. In the summer their conditions are sweaty and smelly. In all seasons they are vulnerable.

When a family is in one room, only one child needs to catch a germ, and the whole family contracts it. Indeed, the situation is worse than this, for if somebody in a multi-occupied house catches something that is particularly contagious, the whole house full of people can catch it. This is not only because of overcrowding, but also the sharing of lavatories, wash basins and dustbins, all places where germs can so easily be picked up.

Nor is the situation helped by the insects or rodents that carry germs with them. And finally, because often the only play space is on the streets, all of the germs that can be picked up from the gutters are brought into the house by the children.

Some recent research in the United States classified the relationship between bad housing and poor health under five headings:

> **"First, acute respiratory infections, because too many people are using the lavatories and bathrooms and because of inadequate heating or ventilation and poor, crowded sleeping arrangements; secondly, certain infectious diseases of childhood (measles, chicken-pox, and whooping cough) have similar causes; thirdly, minor digestive diseases and enteritis are related to poor storage of food and to inadequate washing facilities and lavatories; fourthly, injuries from accidents at home because of crowding or inadequate kitchens or electrical connections and poorly lit unstable stairs; fifthly, diseases of the skin, because of crowding and poor washing facilities."**

Some people may be ill and although one cannot necessarily blame the conditions for causing it, they intensify the misery.

For instance, we found a man in Newcastle, Mr. Evans, who was 56, living in one room on the third floor of a slum house. He was suffering from t.b. but had to climb up three flights of stairs. He shared the lavatory in the yard with eight other people, and in two years in this house his weight fell from 15 to 9 stones. When we walked up the stairs with him, we found the pace demoralisingly slow and he was gasping for breath by the time he reached his room. The Council had been told by a specialist that he must he given a ground floor flat, but at that time there was no sign of it coming.

Another problem is that of mental ill-health. The main sufferers are women, who often become terribly depressed struggling to keep their family together against overwhelming odds. Or become nervy and unstable because of the constant strain.

SHELTER plans a special report on the link between bad housing and overcrowding and physical and mental ill-health, and I don't doubt that it will confirm what two doctors working in the twilight zones told me. The first said that he wrote so many letters to the Housing Director of his local authority that he was better known by him than he was by the local chemists. The second said that he existed "to treat symptoms, instead of the cause". "How can you write out a prescription for a decent home?" he asked me.

The cost in ill-health, and the cost to our health services is part of the price we pay. Hospital beds taken up by people who need not be there if they had a decent room at home. Overworked doctors, and men, women, and children permanently working below their best.

Broken marriages, and neglected children are also part of the price we pay.

Effect on Family Life

I've often wondered how I would cope if I had to keep my family in the housing conditions I've seen in many of our cities. I'm afraid that I could never match the courage and stamina shown by many men and women, nor the way they manage to retain their dignity in conditions that could be expected to turn them into animals.

But, unfortunately but understandably, men do flee the strain and the responsibility, and women do crack up. And children are left to their own devices, in conditions that breed delinquency and crime.

I've never forgotten one day when Richard Holloway, who now runs the Castle Rock Housing Association in Edinburgh, but was at the time working in the Gorbals in

Glasgow, showed me a case in the Gorbals of 54 people living in three flats, comprising four rooms in each flat. In the first was a family of ten, a family of seven, and an old man. In the second was a family of six, a family of three, another family of six, an elderly couple and a family of four. In the third was a family of six, family of eight, and family of five. I repeat–all on the one floor! All cooked their food on coal fires. There was one cold water tap in each flat. None of the toilets were working and buckets of water had to be taken to the toilet on every visit. There were bugs and rats and the house was in a state of unspeakable squalor–it looked as though it had been shelled. But the most revealing thing about this case is that four of the girls and three of the boys all at different times ran away from the nightmare of living in that overcrowded existence, all of the girls and one of the boys ending up in an approved school, and the other two boys in borstal. All of them being punished by society. All of them in my view, and in Richard Holloway's view, were victims of the housing problem. "It was the place's fault."

Insecurity

Then there is the problem of insecurity, created in the main by fear of eviction or the threat of eviction. It is one of the chief destroyers of the families that disintegrate and break-up. Any family faced with continual, nerve-racking insecurity is, by any civilised definition, homeless.

Insecurity leads to strain within the family, causing rows and tension and worry.

Insecurity often created by ignorance of rights or fear to exercise rights, can lead people to act rashly or panic when they need not, simply because the strain of living with uncertainty is worse than knowing exactly where they stand–often in the street!

The 1965 Rent Act (later incorporated in the 1968 Rent Act) was supposed to bring an end to insecurity. The

Minister of Housing at that time, Richard Crossman, said:

> **"Anybody who is the rightful occupier of a house in the broadest sense will from now on be protected against people who bully them, people who persecute, people who try to force them to pay a higher rent, or force them to get out of a place. That will become a crime. These people are to be protected throughout the country.**

SHELTER subsequently carried out intensive research into insecurity and established 13 aspects of insecurity that still exist.

In the SHELTER Report on insecurity, "Notice to Quit" a SHELTER researcher wrote this about a family in East London:

> **"One Saturday last year (1967), the landlord decided he wanted to get rid of the family for good, He switched off their gas, electricuty and water, all in rapid succession and refused to put them on again when asked. The family called the police and when they arrived the landlord said he was going to switch off the gas, electricity and water every Saturday. The police warned him he would be asking for trouble. Soon after this, while Mrs. G. was in the kitchen, and her husband elsewhere in the flat, the landlord burst into the kitchen and began to attack Mrs. G., hitting her in the stomach (remember she was pregnant) with his stick (he was semi-crippled). Her husband heard her screams and raced in, throwing the landlord out of the room so that he fell and broke his ankle. Mrs.G. was rushed to hospital for examination and later went to stay temporarily with her mother. They were terrified to go back to the place. Her husband went to stay in a hotel at considerable expense. The Town Clerk's department was prepared to prosecute the landlord and Mrs. G., in fact, took out a summons against him for assault. Shortly afterwards, with the**

> **protection of the police and some friends, they went back to the flat and collected their belongings. Finally, two days before the baby was born, they were rescued by a housing association and dropped the summons for assualt which was due to be heard the same day the baby was born."**

Yet, when introducing legislation, Richard Crossman said:

> **"It is the minimum duty of a civilized society to protect everyone against harassment in his home, and arbitrary eviction."**

It should be emphasised, though, that the real villain is neither the landlord nor the tenant. The real villain is the housing shortage itself. Insecurity of tenure, with all its damaging side-effects, will only disappear when there is an adequate supply of housing for all our people. As long as basic necessities are in short supply, human beings will be open to exploitation, and a few desperate or occasionally evil landlords can get the great majority of decent people a bad name. It is the problem's fault.

Economics of Homelessness

So far I've talked of the social cost of bad housing–ill–health, marital break-up, child neglect, crime and delinquency, and insecurity. But the housing problem also costs us money. It's impossible to work out the cost to the nation of the loss of productivity caused by the tiredness and unfitness of men struggling against slum conditions.

But it costs on average £8.1.9 to keep one child 'in care' for a week. Multiply that by the 7,000 odd children who were believed to be 'in care' on one night recently for housing reasons alone, and you can see that they cost about £50,000 a week, or £2,750,000 a year.

Effect on Equality

But there is another price that we pay for bad housing

and overcrowding, and that is the devastating blow they strike at one of our most universally-shared ideals–that of equality of opportunity.

Equality of opportunity, as understood by most people, relates to education and employment. "If there are plenty of schools and a variety of jobs, there is equality of opportunity for all", the theory goes. And so there would be, if everybody were equally, physically and psychologically, equipped to realise their full potential, either at school or at work.

But the fact is that children do not arrive at school, men and women do not arrive at work, equally fit. And whilst some may be inherently weak, most are made weak by another factor in their lives: poverty, and an inadequate home environment.

Our society is not genuinely competitive at all, because the dice are loaded against a section of the community when the competition begins!

A competitive society is only genuinely competitive if everybody has a genuine chance of winning, and secondly is only worthwhile if the prizes are the luxuries in life–the things we can do without–and not necessities of life.

Again SHELTER has researched this problem thoroughly, and in its special report, "Back to School from a Holiday in the Slums" asked about the children who go to school from slums:

Can school be any more to them than a change of environment?

Are they going to school each day from housing conditions so oppressive that their capacity for education is severely restricted?

Are they, as a result, so handicapped in our competitive society that they are inevitably destined to be the losers?

Is their childhood a time of lost opportunity?

The questions were asked of school teachers and social workers in the slum districts of London and Birmingham, and from an overwhelming majority the answer was a sad affirmative.

I can remember Brian Benjamin, teacher at a comprehensive in North Kensington, saying:

> **"For ten years I have taught the adolescents of this twilight zone and in that time I have witnessed a heartbreaking stream of lost opportunity, of lives ruined before they even truly started."**

A deep sense of despair can be found among teachers, social workers, and parents. The teachers feel they and their pupils are struggling without hope against insurmountable obstacles; the social workers believe that without the variety of experience that is important for intellectual growth, children in poor conditions aren't fit to compete; parents feel deeply distressed about the effect on their children in waking, dressing, washing, eating, living and sleeping with their parents, brothers, and sisters in one room.

Once again there is the health problem.

A Birmingham schoolmistress told us:

> **"Children from poor homes are absent longer; they are full of colds and snivels. And this creates another problem. There is a terrible discrepancy between their home and school life, making it more of an effort if they have been away to get back into the habit of going to school again. This school seems unreal after the reality of home."**

Then there is the problem of tiredness. Social workers say that overcrowded sleeping conditions make children too tired to work at school. I, myself, have seen rooms where three or four children sleep in one bed, and it only needs one to turn over and they all wake up. A teacher told us of one boy:

> **"When he used to fall asleep in the classroom, as he often did, I used to think of the previous evening, of the boy waiting for his parents to retire to their**

> **overcrowded room, so that he could himself get some rest–and I let him sleep."**

The lack of colour and variety in the lives of children living in slum housing has its effect. The effect on one child was summed up by another teacher in Birmingham:

> **"I know of a child of ten living with his mother and father in one room. The kitchen is under the stairs. He is restricted; there is nowhere for him to play. He has no garden at all. He has been living there four or five years, and in those formative years he has developed none of the skills that a child of that age should normally have. He doesn't run about like the other children. He is lethargic, has no athletic skills and no real inclination to win."**

The children are nervous and insecure. Teachers have told us of children going to school on tranquillizers, one little girl having four tranquillizers during the day and two at night because of the strain of the cramped housing she lived in. The nervousness and insecurity, and neurotic nature of many of the children, makes it difficult for them to concentrate.

> **"After several years' experience as a social worker, I learned to recognise children from bad housing conditions by their behaviour; they showed strong signs of insecurity. They are unable to concentrate, restless, and need to be on the move all the time. There is no continuity in what they do. At the playgroups, they keep starting different activities and dropping them again in quick succession. This means they find it difficult to learn anything. They find it difficult to build up a proper relationship and proper communication."**

Another related problem is that of families moving from place to place desperately trying to find a home. Thus one finds the Plowden Report saying:

> **"We saw admission registers whose pages of new**

> **names with so many rapid crossings out told their own story of a migratory population—a high proportion of those who had been long in the school came from crowded down-at-heel homes. The schools unaided cannot provide all the opportunities their pupils deserve, nor create the labour force this country needs."**

The situation becomes worse when the children become old enough to be thinking in terms of G.C.E. At this stage homework is vital, and yet in the kind of housing conditions I am talking about, homework is impossible.

Such things as reading become impossible in overcrowded conditions, where there is every incentive to parents to get the children out of the house and onto the streets, but where the streets are often dangerous, particularly if the family is living high up in the house where the mother can't keep an eye on the children. And in winter, of course, the children are forced to play indoors anyway.

Older children have a further problem in that nearly everything they try to do will be destroyed by the younger ones. Teachers in the twilight zones would tell you that they won't give expensive school books to children to take home, because they get ruined.

Thus a picture builds up of children that are too tired and too sick to benefit properly from their schooling, often absent, moving from school to school, insecure and neurotic and unable to concentrate, lacking the variety of experiences that make them open and receptive to education.

It is a terrifying thought that until recently such children faced tests at the age of eleven to decide what educational opportunities they would get. It's not difficult to guess where the most failures were found, nor do we need to, for the Plowden Report and other reports bear this out.

Even now, far too many children leave school at the age of 15, although they had the potential to go on to better things, simply because they can no longer keep up, and also sometimes because they want to escape from their homes.

Because they left school at 15 they are not properly educated; because they're not properly educated, they can't get a decent job; because they can't get a decent job, they can't earn a decent income, they can't afford a decent house, and so they're trapped in a vicious circle–back where they began–the slum dweller, whose best chance in life was to become a slum dweller.

And in answer to the person who would say "I know somebody who made good for such conditions", I would reply that the infrequency of the exception proves the rule.

It is in this inequality of opportunity that the real tragedy of our housing problem lies.

All of this is the price, the far, far too heavy price, we pay for the existence of our homeless families.

One sometimes wishes that even if we were incapable of looking after other people, we were better at looking after ourselves. For this problem affects us all. It costs *us* money. And those social problems are *our* social problems. The price we would pay for solving the housing problem is nothing compared with the gains we would make.

FOUR

"Let the filth be made sterile. Stop the stench."
"I think it is a bit of an impertinence to solicit alms for an operation of this sort when successive Governments are continually admitting without hindrance the riff raff, palsied, crippled, criminals and others fleeing their countries with the primary object of first getting national assistance for which they have not, and will not pay one iota, and secondly to drain the National Health Funds to the uppermost."
"If niggers are living in slums its their own fault. No one asked them or wanted them to come to our overcrowded island. And get rid of the bloody yid landlords who are making fortunes out of gentile poverty. They took over our property while we were fighting their war for them. What the Germans stopped them doing–taking control of the country–we've allowed them to do. Hitler was right."
"The problem can be cured by stopping all immigrants–white, black, and yellow (this includes heavy breeding Southern Irish) entering Britain, and birth control."
"You can point the finger well and truly at the Home Secretary for allowing heathen immigrants into this country, whores with illegitimate children, Russian writers who are fornicators, and all the riff raff imaginable."
All the above are extracts from letters to the author.

The following telegram and letter were sent to Kenneth Allsop after he made a television appeal for SHELTER:

"YOU MAKE ME TOTALLY SICK KINDLY DO NOT DISH OUT TRASH ON THE B.B.C. FOR AN IDIOT RABID MOB SUCH AS SHELTER OR FOR 24 HOURS WHICH PAYS YOU TO PERFORM AS A PUBLIC IDIOT"

"I was surprised to see that you have chosen to ask for donations to SHELTER. As you have had the nerve to do the commentary for a film on Danish pornography you don't expect us to cough up to feather-bed the rabble you try to increase by your obvious happiness in showing the lower-brained members of our society just how to propagate their species so making a few more "lascars" in need of shelter. You make me sick."

YOU CAN'T HOUSE A FAMILY IN A CONTRACEPTIVE

Not so long ago a doctor in south-west London tore a SHELTER picture of a homeless family out of his newspaper and posted it to me. Attached to it was a contraceptive. This was his own peculiar way of making the point that homeless families with a number of children have, as so many of their critics claim, "only themselves to blame".

No one would suggest that all those who believe that birth control is the only answer to the housing problem, or that we should stop all immigration, are as ill as the people quoted above. But they represent the tip of an iceberg of irrational prejudice.

The best form of defence, if one wants to avoid making some small sacrifice to help others, seems to be to feed on prejudice against them–prejudice against immigrants, against larger families, against the poor who can so easily be pointed to and accused of being "dirty" and "irresponsible." When the majority are under pressure, the temptation is to find scapegoats. Inevitably the scapegoats are the people who don't fit the standards and norms of our society, and are the most vulnerable anyway, for we tend to organise ourselves in such a way that we cater for the majority.

This is to be seen, for instance, in house sizes–a point I referred to earlier. Because the majority believe that two or three children is a sensible and convenient number, the institutions that serve the majority cater for that size of family. The inevitable result is an acute shortage of housing for the larger family, or for the single old person. But having discriminated against the larger family by not creating the housing for it, we then turn on it and say: "Well it's their fault they're homeless–they had too many children."

Larger families

It is important to recognise that larger families are discriminated against, not just in the sense that there are few homes of sufficient size for them, but because the housing subsidy system has been, up to now, so designed as to deter–no doubt unintentionally–even housing associations from providing for them.

Not only is this failing to cater for them, creating the likelihood of the breaking up of larger families with all of the economic and social consequences of that, but it is based on blind allegiance to "the norm" in a society that in fact never will have all of its families of the same size, and would probably be extremely boring if it did.

There will always be larger families, and not to cater for them is socially absurd and unfair.

There are two aspects of this question:

Firstly, should adults have more children than they can adequately provide for?

Secondly, what do we do with the larger families that do exist?

The answer to the first question is that, ideally, no one will have more children than they can properly look after, but, as I've said, to expect this ideal situation to exist is ludicrous.

The simple fact is that many people are just not bright enough to do what is best for themselves. This being the case, instead of automatically pointing the finger of contempt at the family, we might look critically at our local authorities to see how many are developing family planning services under the 1967 Family Planning act. In my view they have failed lamentably in this respect.

Then again, it is unfair and unrealistic to overlook the effect of firm religious beliefs on some families. I'm not a Catholic, but if someone is brought up from childhood to believe that contraception is wrong, and this view is strongly imposed even when he or she becomes an adult, it should be possible to understand the tremendous pressures needed to overcome this before proper family planning is applied.

Thus before condemning larger families, we might do well to see whether we as a society are pulling our weight, both in making the information available, and in creating the climate of opinion that makes family planning a better understood and less feared prospect for many.

But in any event, what do we do when the larger family is there? Surely, the children, having been born, are entitled to the same chance as every other child. They can't be condemned for their choice of parents, for they didn't have that choice. They cannot be condemned for the size of the family, because they couldn't influence it.

Thus prejudice against the larger family, particularly when it turns into a refusal to provide decent housing and reduces equality of opportunity, is punitive and vengeful, as well as totally negative in its consequences.

Family planning can benefit our society tremendously *tomorrow*. It is no help to the children born *today* You can't house a family in a contraceptive! To keep it together, and to give it an equal chance, you have to give it a decent home.

Immigrants

Judging by the post that I receive, the number one scapegoats are the immigrants.

"Send the wogs back and you won't have a housing problem" sums up their views in a nutshell. Many are merely using the housing problem as yet another chance to get at immigrants. Others really do believe that the housing problem is the result of a "flood" of immigrants into the country "bringing the problem with them", and if only they would go away, the problem would miraculously disappear.

The facts just don't bear this argument out; firstly, the problem was there long before immigration rose to the level it did in the late 1950's. But even if the basic premise is accepted, the thesis is not valid, for in 1951 (before the so-called "flood") we had a "crude housing deficit" of nearly a million dwellings, and in 1966 (after the "flood") the deficit was running at only 210,000. Now a "crude surplus" is being forecast.

Nor has the U.K. population in fact been increased by immigration—more people have left Britain than come into it in the majority of years since the War! Between 1964 and 1968 342,400 more people left the U.K. than entered.

Now though it's impossible to look at housing in complete isolation, and even if immigrants do in some areas appear to intensify the housing problem, one must balance the problems they solve against the problems they may or may not cause. Immigrants undertake many of the poorly-paid service jobs in our larger cities, and they tend to be the victims and not the agents of years of neglect of our housing stock.

To say they have taken away council houses overlooks clear discrimination against immigrants by many councils. For instance, in Wolverhampton immigrants have to satisfy longer residential qualifications that others on council waiting lists.

They have also suffered from discrimination when trying to get mortgages, or move out of decaying cities, and in a variety of other ways.

The Milner Holland Committee said;

> **"As newcomers to London, they find just because they are newcomers and also because they tend to move about from one area to another, that they have very low priority for obtaining local authority housing; they have no residential qualifications for any housing list, where this is required. At the same time, they are needed to man many of the metropolitan services."**

The Centre for Urban Studies, reporting on North Kensington, said:

> **"It is just these people on the move from places near and far who are required to meet local labour shortages in services and other industries; and in all the unskilled and skilled occupations, they keep the metropolitan machine running. Indeed, the very people who are not wanted on the local housing market are needed for the local labour market.**

As in so many other aspects of the structure of British society, immigrants have highlighted inadequacies in the structure from which they have suffered directly, and then, to add insult to injury, have been accused of causing the inadequacy.

Among other things, they are accused (as you can see from the letters that open this chapter) of using more than their share of the social service expenditure, yet the evidence is that they use £13.7 less in social service expenditure per capita than the population as a whole.

They are accused of "coming here to live off the dole" and yet 66% of the immigrant population contribute to the national labour force, as opposed to 50% of the home born population.

One has tried to meet the anti-immigrant group on the basis of the facts, but there is a moral position as well. Whether we were right or wrong to allow them to come to the country is irrelevant once they are here. The immigrants *are* here, and *are* citizens of this country. In any just society all of its citizens, whatever colour, and wherever they were born, should be entitled to the basic necessities of life–food, clothing, a decent home, and equality of opportunity.

Problem Families

Yes they do exist. To pretend that there are not families with multiple problems, that there are not men or women who are weak-willed and largely responsible for their own circumstances, would be to strain the credibility of my readers.

I will simply make three points from my experience:

Firstly, the problem families that become homeless are far outnumbered by the number of homeless families that become problems. In the majority of cases the difficulties of the so-called "problem family" are either caused or intensified by a record of insecurity and bad housing.

Secondly, despite the ill-effect of bad housing of the number of families that are homeless, only a minority could be called problem families.

Thirdly, where a family *is* a problem because of inherent

weaknesses in the character of one or both of the parents, but where it is in the interests of the people concerned–both adults and children–to live together as a family and draw strength from family life, society only hurts itself by trying to punish them through homelessness. Apart from cheating itself of any chance of solving the family's problems, society fools itself if it thinks the families will just disappear. The people will still be there, and ultimately will still be society's responsibility.

One of the weaknesses of our society is that it's ready to show compassion for the groups that most obviously deserve it–the old, the sick, and the needy–until it becomes a kind of political jingoism of need, but is reluctant to show pity for the less obviously pitiful.

Our compassion tends to be skin deep, in that we care most when we can clearly see that somebody has been handicapped in the same way that "but for good fortune" we too could have been handicapped. We are compassionate, for instance, towards the blind because we know we were fortunately born with sight and that if we were blind we would need to be helped.

But the test of a compassionate society is the response it shows to the needs of the *undeserving* poor. What about the morally disabled? The weak willed? How does our compassion measure up to their needs? Usually it doesn't. Although we concede it might be possible for us to be physically handicapped, it seems inconceivable to the majority that they could ever be morally weak. For the weak-willed our society finds little but contempt. In fact, we punish the weak-willed by a system of material deprivation.

In this reaction, we are not only lacking in compassion, but our policy is both economically and socially unsound. And we deny the real nature of the disease. It can sometimes be harmless, but often in a competitive and demanding society it can be crippling, and even fatal. At its worst, to be weak-willed is to suffer from a form of disablement, for it means that a man has no more control over some aspects of his life than a cripple might have over his arms or legs. In an extreme form, it means that the mind of a man can argue forcibly and logically that he should go in one direction, while his legs take him in another. In its usual form, moral weakness is seen in the failure of a man to resist successfully the powerful pull of the variety of temptations our society has put within his reach.

If the weakness is a minor one–maybe as simple as a compulsion to watch television every hour of the day or night–it's possible that only the victim will be affected.

But if his weakness is gambling, or drink, or he is a compulsive spendthrift, and he has a family and a home, then the repercussions of his weakness can amount to a catastrophe in family and social as well as personal terms. And in our response to that we are all too often exposed as a society that, rather than being compassionate, is pitiless and vengeful.

The answer to this problem is not an easy one, but if we as a society recognise that being weak-willed can be so in-bred in a man's character that he has been born disabled, our attitudes to his problems might not only be better for him, and his family, but also for society itself.

Sometimes, though, one has to help a family where one would instinctively like to walk out. I can remember going with a housing association social worker to visit an elderly couple who had pleaded for rehousing, because they were living in a basement room and the only lavatory was up a 17-step stairway. The old lady–she was in her sixties–was a cripple and rarely made it to the top in time.

When we got there we found that the man was near to being a monster, bad tempered and shouting at the poor old lady, although she was incapable of helping herself. Her life was clearly a misery, and the man's arrogance when we called was calculated to alienate anyone. He swore at us and ignored his wife's timid expression of hope that we might be able to help. In the end, we nearly fell over backwards to persuade him to accept the home that many another couple would have leapt at. Why? Because no matter how much one disliked the man, that woman desperately needed a gesture of friendship, and desperately needed a more comfortable home.

Likewise, one often helps the family despite finding it extremely difficult to be sympathetic to the father, simply because there are children who are entitled to consideration as individuals. Even if one dislikes the parents, can one ignore four or five little individuals whose characters are being formed or malformed by the conditions they have been brought into, through no fault of their own.

Yes, problem families do exist. No, they do not offer any way out for the rest of society, for though they may be welfare problems they offer no excuse for not solving the housing problem.

Isolation

Prejudice has its origins in fear and in ignorance.

As long as there is economic and environmental poverty on a large scale we cannot hope to tackle effectively the problem of racial prejudice. For two million families living in Britain on or near the poverty line the fear of losing out in the race for the necessities of life–food, clothing, education and a decent home–creates for them what they believe to be a justification for standing on anybody to reach the first rung of the ladder to prosperity, and those they can most easily isolate are those who are a different colour.

It's crazy–but can we really blame them? And can we blame the black man in our society if he rebels against being crippled by poverty, and by the lack of a decent base for his life operation?

Moral stands on race are one thing. Practical steps to solve the problems of race are another. Thus we should attack the social problems that breed despair and violence and prejudice—we should attack them, as the U.S. Riot Commission were told: "because there is simply no other way to achieve a decent and orderly society".

But the problems I have been talking about in this chapter also owe a lot to ignorance. For poverty in an affluent society, and we *are* on the whole an affluent society, is also isolation.

This isolation brings a failure to understand what it is that the poor and the homeless have to overcome. It leads to a preparedness by people to judge others from an unequal standpoint.

No one has the right to judge others, unless from an understanding of their circumstances.

That's why I could never point to a child's dirty face and say: "That mother doesn't care." I know far too many families who get their only water from a cold water tap two or three landings below their meagre little room.

I find it hard to blame a man for going out and drinking when I know that, if I had to return to the same conditions as he does, I would probably run away.

I find it hard to blame a mother because her family looks ragged, because I know that she may have to choose between paying the rent to avoid eviction, or feeding and clothing the family in the way she would like.

Part of this isolation is an inability to share things that other people take for granted. Take Christmas. For the mother of a really poor family, Christmas just underlines the failure of her and her husband to keep up with the rest of us. While other mothers look forward to the excitement of Christmas Day, the homeless mother sneaks away to jumble sales to buy other people's cast off toys; not for her family a turkey—more likely, a cheap joint bought on Christmas Eve. For them Christmas is also winter and winter is a time of dampness, and expense of electricity and gas bills. And worst of all, the dread of the day when the children will go back to school to compare the "load of jumble" they got in their Christmas stockings with the bigger, brighter, brand new presents that their luckier school friends cannot wait to show.

Our gaiety, our momentary goodwill, our gluttony, simply underline their isolation, intensify their bitterness, and harden their hearts against the society they live in.

And we? Our failure to understand is reflected in little things—like our attitude, for instance, to the existence in a slum room of a television set. It is just too easy to jump to the assumption that if they did not possess a television set they might not be in a slum. This is just not realistic while there is an acute scarcity of housing (some families would go without even if we were all millionaires) but anyway the fact is that a television set, while it may be on the fringe of our existence, is central to theirs.

For a family living in one room a television set can sometimes be the one thing that keeps them from going mad. It's a focal point, it's a unifying factor, it's a form of escape, and insomuch as it takes the strain off personal relations it reduces tension, and it can bring a little peace into what is little better than a prison cell where particularly in winter with its long, dark nights, people feel trapped like animals.

And a television set is even more important than that. In a society that is dependent on its communications media it is the ultimate in communications, and to be cut off from television is to be deprived of an advantage that the majority possess. It can also be a social disadvantage not to have a television set, for so many people do have one—particularly working-class people—that television has itself become an everyday topic of conversation, and the man or woman without a television set can often feel left out because they are, firstly, not up to date with what is going on, and secondly, not able to discuss programmes with their friends or workmates.

In other words, not only do we, through our isolation, fail to understand why the poor have to have their television set, but if the poor do not have that television set, they are even more isolated.

Yet you would be amazed at the number of people who say to me: "If they can afford a television set they can afford a home."

I know there will be people who will say: "Well, for heaven's sake, there are children in Africa and Asia starving to death and your're talking about whether or not children should have a television set."

But this is a reflection on the enormous gap between the privileged countries and the under-privileged countries. If we live in a privileged society, we cannot point to the under-privileged in our society and say they must be the people who pay for our consciences. It is the majority, and those who prosper, who must pay so that the difference between privilege and under-privilege can be reduced, whether it be between nations, or between communities.

Relative poverty is just as crippling as absolute poverty. and sometimes can be crueller. At least in a poor society, there is communal suffering, with all the understanding and all the joint effort that that brings. But in an affluent society, the poor must not only overcome their poverty, but the lack of understanding and prejudice of the majority.

In my speeches over the past three years I have often quoted the words of Martin Luther King who, speaking at the end of the Civil Rights March, in Washington in 1963, said of the American negroes:

> "They live isolated on a lonely island of poverty in an ocean of material prosperity."

In my view a substantial number of people in Britain live

so isolated environmentally, so isolated economically, and so isolated socially, that they might just as well be living in a lonely island in the English Channel for all that they share of what the majority take for granted.

The challenge that exists for our society is whether the majority are going to devote their energies and their education, which at the present time they have at the expense of a minority, to building up the walls of the fortress on the mainland, or to building a bridge between that island and the mainland and properly integrating all of our citizens into society by giving them genuine equality of opportunity.

FIVE

"What is it we really want?
For what end and how?
If it is something feasible, obtainable,
Let us dream it now,
And pray for a possible land . . ."

Louis McNeice, "Autumn Journal"

A POSSIBLE LAND

Involvement in the SHELTER campaign in the past four years has not been merely participation in housing, but in the running of the "casualty ward". Confronted day-by-day with families breaking up, and with the housing problem at its most acute, it would be forgiveable if we became depressed, and pessimistic. Surprisingly, I live in hope.

I believe that a Britain without a housing problem *is* a possible land—that we *can* solve the housing problem within a decade, leaving only the self-perpetuating problem caused by fresh need, obsolescence, and rising expectation.

We *can* afford to do it. The resources are there both in terms of money and manpower. After all, compared with most other countries in the world, we are affluent, and the near phenomenal rise to prominence of the SHELTER movement has shown that the will to solve the problem exists among many of our people.

On the surface the will exists among our politicians as well. Note the following:

> **"First among the priorities of the Seventies is to get rid of the scandal of bad housing and no-housing. That is why all of us here are on the same side as SHELTER."**
>
> *Harold Wilson, Labour Party Conference, 1969.*

> **"The next Conservative Government will give high priority to the problems of the homeless. We have already agreed to redefine the homeless and to make a genuine endeavour to redefine the problem properly."**
>
> *Conservative Leader, Edward Heath, March 19, 1970.*

> **"The worst social evil in this country is bad housing . . . I therefore urge Liberals to make the scandal of bad housing a major political issue; and I repeat my demands for action . . ."**
>
> *Liberal Leader, Jeremy Thorpe,*
> *Liberal Party Assembly, 1969.*

If words were homes, every family in Britain would be living in a castle. But the history of housing in this country is a melancholy catalogue of broken promises, from Lloyd George's "homes fit for heroes", to Harold Wilson's "500,000 houses a year by 1970".

Unfortunately, in Britain political priority is just as likely to mean prior claim to attention in party propaganda as it is to mean prior claim in terms of resources.

To the broken promises, can be added irresponsible prophecy. The answer to the housing problem, we were told, always lay just around the corner, and effort has always been restricted on the basis that we might be in danger of excess provision.

The Labour administration inherited in 1964 a grim legacy of poverty, housing squalor, and social oppression from many years of Conservative administration, and though one can criticise many aspects of the Labour performance, it would ill-benefit the Conservatives, on the basis of their record in the past, and what they are doing at local level today, to complain too loudly.

Just as the Child Poverty Action Group, dominated by Labour supporters, has been accused of disloyalty for its vocal criticism of Labour's performance in relieving poverty, so have the members of the SHELTER movement–at least those who do have Labour sympathies–been similarly accused.

But the pressure of organisations like SHELTER can and should be a source of strength to Ministers, for they give them additional weight when they go into the Cabinet Room to fight for their share of Government resources. The housing problem will not be solved by under-estimating what remains to be done, and if one is tough on a Labour administration that has, to be fair, done so much better than its predecessors, it is as much in sorrow as in anger.

The Labour administration has, though, claimed much credit for its housing record since1965, and one has no choice but to put it in the context of the on-going problem.

Let's look at just a few of the main pegs in the Labour housing programme:

1. Overall Scarcity

This was to be tackled by a greatly increased housing programme, building up to 500,000 new homes a year by 1970. In 1967 a record of 404,356 houses were completed, and this record was broken in 1968, the figure becoming 413,715. But in 1969 their target was abandoned, and only 366,793 were built, with a similar number expected in 1970.

In the Report of the Ministry of Housing 1967/8 the Minister said:

> **"The results over the two year period must be looked at against the economic measures taken at the end of 1967 and during 1968. Devaluation and the other measures associated with it were announced in November, 1967. Following this, in January, 1968, the Government decided to make reductions in the public authority house building programme below the level previously planned in each of the years 1968 and 1969."**

In other words, the Minister was admitting that it was a Government decision to reduce public authority house-building, and this makes his criticism of Conservative councils less valid.

Again in the same Report he said:

> **"The decision to reduce the public sector programme after devaluation made it no longer realistic to think in terms of 500,000 new houses completed in the U.K. in 1970."**

This was a clear admission both of the abandonment of the target and that it was his decision to cut back council house building.

Labour further alleged that the need for the target no longer existed, both because of the potential housing surplus, and because of greater emphasis on rehabilitation.

But rehabilitation will take a long time to make its impact, and cannot be accepted as a valid reason for cutting back new building. Even the Labour Party's own study group agrees with this.

Indeed, one of the strongest arguments for rehabilitation is that it helps to increase the housing stock, by saving old houses whilst new ones are built. But this worthy object has been defeated because the money to finance rehabilitation has been taken from money previously allotted for new building.

The thinking here is obvious: if we're saving a lot more older houses, we don't need to build so many new ones. Thus, we can solve the problem without boosting resources. This, if there were no urgency involved, might stand up as an argument, but it overlooks the need for housing *now*.

Why should we always be so terrified of the danger of having too many houses? It seems to me a far more desirable fate than always to have insufficient.

2. Emphasis on council houses

Another peg of the Labour programme was to give priority to council house building, and in the year 1967 completions in the public sector went up to 203,918, compared with 200,438 in the private sector. But by 1968 completions in the private sector had taken the lead again, going up by 20,000 while in the public sector they fell by over 10,000.

Equally serious, even where council houses were built, rising rents were making them too expensive for the poorest families.

3. Security

One of the main pegs in the Labour programme was to end insecurity and exploitation in privately rented property, with the 1965 Rent Act, later consolidated in the 1968 Rent Act.

And yet SHELTER's report, "Notice to Quit", exposed 13 areas of insecurity in housing in 1968.

Families in furnished tenancies could still be evicted through a relatively simple process. Defenders of this situation argued that if the Rent Act was extended to furnished flats, people would be discouraged to let, and the accommodation available would be further reduced. But, as things were, the Rent Act, from the point of view of security, might just as well not have existed in overcrowded areas, for landlords simply made all their tenancies furnished.

Harassment continued, for the tenant often found his case difficult to prove and, even if he won, he still had to live with the insecurity created by growing hostility from the landlord.

Families were still being illegally forced to leave, sometimes without notice, and others tricked into going.

Some landlords were even prepared to risk prosecution and a fine for harassment in the knowledge that whether the tenant won or lost his case, he would probably go in the end and the average fine for harassment was laughable compared with the additional income obtainable when the tenant was out. (One landlord, because he could sell with vacant possession, sold a house at an extra £1,500. When this is compared with the average fine for harassment it's possible to see why some landlords are prepared to regard prosecution as merely part of the cost of operating a profitable enterprise. For instance, between December 8, 1965, and March 31, 1968, there were 714 summonses for such offences. Only 60 of the 408 fines exceeded £50 and only four offenders were sent to prison. The maximum fine for a first offence is £100.)

For many families a visit to the Rent Tribunal was proving the first step towards homelessness; landlords make their dislike of such action quite clear and often the result has been harassment and legal or illegal evictions.

The Rent Act had done nothing to help the insecure in tied accommodation–that is to say where the house is tied to a particular job. This kind of tenant was even more insecure, for if he lost his job he lost his home at the same time.

Protests were made by SHELTER, and many other people, over a long time and the Labour administration remained remarkably insensitive to them until late in 1969 when Anthony Greenwood finally set up the Francis Committee to look at how the Rent Act was working. While this was at least an advance one can only regret that the Labour administration, whilst securely in power, did not do more to tighten up all exploitation of homelessness in areas of acute housing stress.

4. Regional Development

A fourth peg in the Labour administration's programme was to put even greater stress on building up the regions, with inducement to industry to move there, and the stemming of office and industrial expansion in overcrowded areas like the south-east and West Midlands. A new town programme was planned. The thinking here, again, was good, but the leadership uninspired. Thus, in late 1969 the "Face the Facts" report stated that the crucial south-east new towns policy was in disarray.

5. Home Ownership

Big efforts were made to bring home ownership within the grasp of more families, with the introduction of the option mortgage scheme, and encouragement to local authorities to give home loans. Home loan finance for councils reached a figure of £191 million by 1965/66 but then was scandalously allowed to drop to only £30 million, and then gradually increased to just over £150 million in mid-1970. Local authorities could only operate a stop-go-stop policy in distributing loans, and at a time when new breeds of home owner had been emerging, this inconsistency of Government encouragement was deplorable.

And so, a Labour administration that had begun so well—by boosting the new building, by concentrating on the needs of poorer families, by tackling the problems of insecurity, by facing up to the need for building up the regions, and by encouraging home ownership, had allowed all these aspects of its housing programme to decline.

Why did it happen?

At the time of writing the General Election was only a

few weeks away and I believe that Labour could have gone into it with a proud housing record, and showing believable promise, if it had not been for three things:

1. The cutback in resources

Probably Harold Wilson had no idea of the effect of a lapse of effort in just one year, but in terms of undermining all of the best in the housing programme, the cutbacks after devaluation were disastrous. It was also in defiance of the Prime Minister's promise at the time of devaluation:

> **"We are cutting public expenditure–including the capital outlay on the nationalised industries. There will be cuts in local authority expenditure . . . But while, in crisis programme after crisis programme announced by right hon. Gentlemen opposite, local authority, housing, school building– and their mini-programme for hospitals–were cut, the housing programme, the school building programme, the hospital building programme, will continue to expand in accordance with the priorities we have laid down."**

It is a tragedy that the Minister did not fight harder, or that the Chancellor was not more sympathetic.

2. Lack of Leadership

Some Ministries require administration and some require leadership. In housing the priority need is for the latter, and Anthony Greenwood, no matter how sincere he might have been, was conspicuously ineffective. There has been a discouraging faith in legislation alone, and a failure to see that if legislation, such as the 1969 Housing Act, is to become a reality, it has to be carried out with nothing less than crusading zeal.

3. Failure to tackle housing subsidies

In failing to grasp the nettle of an antiquated system of

housing subsidies, the Administration has also failed to create the conditions essential to the effective working of most of its programme.

A possible answer

We can do better. But how?

The emphasis in this book is understandably on the existence of the problem, and of the work of SHELTER in tackling it. But it would be cowardly of me not to put forward a few thoughts on how the problem might be solved.

To sum up in a nutshell, I believe in a balanced housing programme, injected with greater resources, and a note of real urgency, and based on a radical overhaul of out-of-date approaches, particularly to housing subsidies.

In particular, I would advocate the following nine steps:

1. Minister of Housing and Land

Following on the creation of an overlord for housing, transport, and environmental matters, I would continue this a stage further, by making a Minister responsible for the housing programme only–Minister of Housing and Land.

Such Minister would be able to clear the decks and tackle this major problem without having his energies diverted, thus providing the really single-minded leadership required.

One can't over-exaggerate the need for leadership. This goes far beyond bullying and cajoling local authorities to boost new building. The rehabilitation programme is dependent on inspired leadership, for so much voluntary participation is called upon from owner-occupiers, landlords, tenants, local authorities, and everybody concerned with urban affairs. Leadership is essential if tenants are to get to know their rights. Leadership is essential to appreciation of the fresh initiatives being taken on the fringes of the housing field, some of them with dazzling potential. Real courage is required to force through the radical changes in housing subsidies that are urgently needed.

Housing is the single field where there is the most opportunity for participation by all our people and the Minister of Housing tackling the problem with compassion and determination; rolling up sleeves, and taking much of the political squabbling out of housing, could bring real hope into a field bedevilled by a combination of party politics and Ministerial and public lethargy for far too long.

2. Resources

A problem as complicated as housing will not be solved by money alone, but nor will it be solved without it.

When the Labour Party came to power it said in the White Paper of 1965:

> **"The U.K. record has in recent years been almost the worst . . . the evidence suggests that the most successful housebuilding countries lead the U.K. at least partly because they have chosen to devote a greater proportion of their national resources and their capital investment to housing . . ."**

Look then at the table on next page:

Percentage of Gross National Product devoted to house building in Western Europe. (Public and private)
(U.N. Economic Commission for Europe: 'Annual Bulletin of Housing and Building Statistics for Europe' 1967 & 1968.)

The figures speak for themselves—we've only fractionally increased the percentage of the G.N.P. devoted to housing, and slipped from second–last position among the recorded Western European countries to last position.

Private investment, too, must be stimulated.

One way to do this might be to encourage the public to invest in housing by the selling of housing bonds, tax free, with a return of 5%. Thus the investor can play an

Rank			%
1967	1	Greece	6.8
	2	Sweden	6.4
	3	Switzerland	6.3
	4	France	6.2
	5	Italy	6.1
	6	Finland)	
		Netherlands)	5.7
	7	West Germany	5.2
	8	Belgium)	
		Portugal)	
		Austria)	5.0
	9	Denmark	4.7
	10	Norway	4.4
	11	Ireland	4.2
	12	U.K.	3.7

Rank			%
1958-67	1	Switzerland	6.6
	2	Italy	6.5
	3	Greece	6.4
	4	France	5.5
		West Germany	
	5	Sweden	5.4
	6	Belgium)	
		Finland)	
		Austria)	5.0
	7	Netherlands	4.6
	8	Norway	4.2
	9	Denmark	3.7
	10	Portugal	3.5
	11	U.K.	3.2
	12	Ireland	2.9

invaluable role in helping others, and at the same time get a return. To underline the social benefit of a housing bonds programme, the money raised could be restricted to a limited number of projects, not least the provision of 100% home loans to poorer sections of the community, both to help them become home owners and to boost investment in older property.

In addition, building societies who boost interest rates whenever the bank rate goes up, should be compelled to reduce them at the same level when the bank rate goes down.

Still on the question of resources, ways must be created of helping those who can't afford decent housing to pay for it, and this involves both the revision of the housing subsidy system, and the boosting of the incomes of lower paid workers.

Only by paying people more can we guarantee they will

be able to afford the basic necessities of life, and in this respect you cannot disassociate housing from the incomes policy.

But in any event, we can no longer postpone an overhaul of our crazy and chaotic system of housing subsidies–a system that has no justice and that isolates one group on no rational basis; a system that gives rent protection to some and not to others; a system that encourages rent rebate schemes but does not enforce their use; a system that allows rents to vary for comparable housing in neighbouring boroughs; a system that makes council rents go up disproportionately to increases in incomes in order that old loans to the council can be renewed at higher interest rates; a system that cannot see the difference between a rich and a poor local authority.

At its worst, it subsidises bricks and mortar, instead of people, and a situation is created where the owner-occupier is subsidised through the tax system, and the council tenant is subsidised through Exchequer subsidies to local authorities, but the tenant of the private landlord gets no help from either the rate payer or the Exchequer.

Thus, you can find in an inner London Borough two families:

The first is a tenant of a private landlord, a family of five living in one room without the comforts we take for granted–without hot water, kitchen, bathroom, or room to move, and sharing a cold water tap and lavatory. The house is badly maintained and they're plagued by ill-health that they blame on the dampness, on inadequate plumbing and a damaged roof. They pay £5 a week for what is laughingly called "furnished" housing.

Nearby, a family of five paying £3.14.0. plus rates for a council house, with kitchen, bathroom, living room, and three bedrooms, on a recently built estate.

Incredibly, the first family is not only paying an excessive rent, without security, but also helping to pay through rates and taxes for the housing of the second. Yet the income of the second is slightly higher than the income of the first.

An overhaul of the whole system is becoming a matter of great urgency and any Minister of Housing with courage and determination wouldn't have any alternative but to do it, and to do it in one bold and drastic move.

If this were done, and housing resources were boosted, not only would new money come into housing, but much more could be done with the money that is already there.

A lot of "cleaning up" of existing low-cost housing could be done by energetically tackling the problem of under-occupation in council housing, offering worthwhile incentives to people to make way for larger families. In addition a suggestion put forward by Harry Richardson, Director of the Centre for Research in the Social Sciences, and Joan Vipond, lecturer in economics at the University of Kent, is worth considering. They recommend giving £500 (with regional variation) cash grants to council tenants to help them buy their own home, working on the basis that 17% of tenants have a household income greater than £40 and were potential house purchasers. They say:

> **"Under the proposed scheme, the maximum cost of the subsidy would be £384 millions (if the marginal income were £30 per week the maximum cost would be £845 million). If the subsidy payments were spread over a decade–they might in practice be spread over a longer period–the annual cost would vary in the range of 38–84 million pounds. This does not seem excessive compared with annual housing subsidies of £227 million–and personal expenditure of £3,284 millions on rent, rates and maintenance (both 1968). Even so subsidisation on this scale of relatively well-off groups in the community might be objected to on equity grounds. Our answer to this is**

> **pragmatic. Under this proposal, each £50 millions spent frees 100,000 local authority houses for families in need. The measure would enable local authorities to increase their rate of slum clearance without having to neglect the problems of the homeless and poorer households on the waiting lists. The subsidy costs are small in return for a solution to the country's housing problem."**

Now whether this is the best scheme that can be thought up, I don't know. But clearly a move to the concept of encouraging home ownership, a new form of subsidy–a direct grant towards a deposit–is one that should be considered.

3. Research

A new single-minded Minister of Housing, with more resources, cannot afford to make the mistake of spending them where they are not needed. In order to ascertain just what the housing programme should be, and to create the legislative means, and define the roles of the public, private, and voluntary sectors, so that the manpower is there, the Minister would need to define the housing problem accurately, and base his definition on indisputable information.

One hesitates to recommend a Royal Commission for on no account could it be allowed to hold up the initial steps that must be taken if the housing programme is to move ahead rapidly.

But, on the other hand, if we are to avoid having another "housing surplus" and housing problem at the same time, we need more extensive research, and more public discussion on the implications of the information that becomes available.

An on-going programme of research and enquiry is essential, and this could be backed up by a special, permanent Commission, meeting regularly and publicly, receiving full reports and making recommendations on the basis of the information.

The research, and the collation and interpretation of information, may not appear an exciting beginning to a housing programme, but the inadequacy of such activities in the past are reflected in the chaos that exists today. The lesson is there to be learned.

4. Manpower

At the present time there is growing controversy over who should be providing the houses. Politically, the left are all for massive expansion of the public sector, and the right for rapid expansion of the private sector. This is crazy at a time of acute scarcity, for there is need for maximum effort by everyone.

If the workload is to be spread intelligently, rational conditions created for the distribution of incentives, and firmer direction of the housing programme made possible, then there must be a clearer definition of the roles of the three sectors.

This involves more planning in housing, and not less, and is a rejection of the views expressed by right-wingers, led by Mr. Enoch Powell, who want planning taken out of housing, and a free market to operate.

Thus, they apply the same criteria to the provision of a basic necessity of life, as to the luxuries of life, and in effect say that where there is acute scarcity of the basic necessity, what is available should be thrown onto the open market and human need exploited to the full.

Professor David Donnison, in a 1963 Paper, said:

"Industrial development and the spread of affluence, it is said, will in time provide adequate housing for all but the most unfortunate, feckless or fertile. But growing wealth is not spread evenly, like jam, across the whole country; but it is heavily concentrated in the expanding regions, amongst those who work, and on those with the scarcest skills and the strongest

> **bargaining positions. These are the people who will be able to pay the rising costs of better housing. If left undirected and uncontrolled, the process of enrichment will not remove but sharpen the inequality—inequalities between regions, between a working population and the old, between the skilled and the unskilled—which already lie at the root of our problems. One after another, European countries on both sides of the Iron Curtain have found that a rapid rate of economic growth calls for more, not less, Government intervention in the field of housing."**

Likewise Lord Harlech, Honorary Chairman of SHELTER, speaking in May, 1969 in London said:

> **"I believe there was a time when many economists and social scientists both here and in America believed that a steady expansion of the country's wealth would bring an almost automatic cure to our urban problems. Per capita income would increase, poverty would largely disappear and rents could be charged at a level which would generate a sufficient supply of homes. But what has happened? In America the general standard of living has more than tripled in a generation. It has gone up almost 70% in the last nine years. Yet almost the same proportion of the population is in dire poverty and the conditions in many parts of their cities have continued to deteriorate. All are now agreed that a specially tailored and major assault has got to be made on America's urban ills if their whole society is not to tear itself to pieces."**

The main fallacy in the Powellite's case is that they base their assault on the housing problem entirely on rent levels, in the naive belief that the housing problem is only one of scarcity. But the scarcity today is a problem specially related to the places where people have to live in order to get work, and where there is little available land, and colossal slum clearance requirements–problems that will not be solved by just raising the rent.

We need planning not just to get jobs and houses in the right place, but to get them of the right size, and adequate to meet rising demands. Most important, we need control over the use of land, and careful direction of the various sectors so that they can all thrive, and at the same time meet the social needs of the country.

All of this emphasis on planning should leave the reader in no doubt that I believe the firm direction should come from the Minister of Housing.

He must accumulate the facts about the problem and decide where resources must be concentrated.

He must devise incentives related to the fresh situation, and make them available.

He must link housing to other economic and social factors.

He must provide aid to local authorities who have a disproportionate share of the problem.

It has always been my view that it was a disastrous mistake to pass so much of the housing responsibility of London over to the London Boroughs in 1963. As the Milner Holland Report said:

> **"Not all boroughs will be able to solve their problems alone. In particular, land will be needed in the outer areas and outside London to receive persons displaced from inner areas. If the attack on shortage and bad housing conditions is to be successful, it must be planned applied and directed for London as a whole."**

There is nothing more absurd than to see some inner-London boroughs jealously hanging on to every little bit of power they can get, and at the same time bitterly complaining about the disproportionate share of poverty and bad housing they have to carry.

Real leadership is needed in the London context, and the bickering between the Labour-controlled central administration, and the Tory-controlled G.L.C. has got to stop, and some kind of constructive basis for co-operation be established. While they play politics, the hopes of the homeless descend to an all-time low.

While on the question of the three sectors, I feel there is no alternative but to rule out the role of the private landlord as a provider of homes for lower income groups in our larger cities. Many people argue that the private landlord has been driven out by rent restrictions, but the fact of the matter is that it is beyond the wit of the private landlord to make provision in the overcrowded parts of our cities at a price that the needy can afford. It's a fact of 1970 life. The sooner it's faced up to, the better. Then housing associations could be given their most creative role, with local authorities helping them to buy up whole streets. In cities where the houses are suitable for one family only, home-ownership should be encouraged.

Space doesn't allow me to go into the possible role of each sector, but I do believe that a rationalisation of the situation, and then firm aid and direction to each of the sectors in house provision, is long overdue. In the words of the Milner Holland Committee, the remedy lies "in a common frame of mind. Housing has for too long been the sport of political prejudice".

5. Priority Programme

If one is knocked over in the street and injured quite badly, one is rushed to hospital and immediate emergency action takes place to keep one alive. When this is satisfactorily achieved, then the long-term action is taken to bring one back to full health. A surgical operation followed by a medical operation.

This is what we need in housing.

In addition to a permanent on-going programme, aimed at keeping the nation properly housed, we need a special programme to tackle the problem where it is worse, and to save as many families as possible from years of living in slums or worse.

Britain's housing problem may be nation-wide but at its worst it is a series of blackspots, related to economic strength or industrial expansion.

And so if it is really intended to make housing the number one priority, there should be a dual housing programme.

I would divide the priority areas into two:

Firstly, there would be the areas of acute housing stress, where many of the homeless have to stay because that is where they are, and also will be, needed to work.

Secondly, I would declare as priority housing areas those of potential industrial expansion and development, and link to extra housing provision in those areas other residential incentives, including the creation of attractive recreational facilities. Every effort must be made to boost the wider distribution of industry with even greater incentives.

This priority area campaign should be aimed at building the maximum number of new houses in the minimum number of areas as quickly as possible and would need to be pushed through with ruthless determination. But it would not all be new building–in the same cities the rehabilitation made possible by the Housing Act 1969 would be made workable by the creation of incentives and by the encouragement of urban coalition.

Before one moves on to rehabilitation, one should acknowledge that a priority area programme of a sort already exists, but in my view the number of priority areas–135–is so far in excess of what an emergency programme could sustain that one could not defend Ministerial interpretation of the word "priority".

6. Rehabilitation

Rehabilitation is an extremely worthwhile concept for a number of reasons: firstly, every old house saved makes a new house somewhere else a genuine addition to the housing stock, not merely a replacement; secondly, it's often cheaper; thirdly, you can often keep more families in rehabilitated older properties than you can house on the same land if you demolish and build again; fourthly, it's possible by rehabilitation not only to keep communities together, but actually to foster community spirit.

The first major step has been taken with the 1969 Housing Act, but what is needed is a tremendous injection of money, and willpower, into the improvement area programme. A new and exciting role for private enterprise could be created here in partnership with local authorities and voluntary organisations. Urban coalitions, properly financed, could save whole sections of our cities, and also create a unique role for the people of the area to be involved themselves.

Once again we come back to the ability of people to pay, for the whole concept will collapse unless the lower income groups are helped either to pay rising rents, or to purchase the house they live in. The alternative is that they will be pushed out of their existing communities when rehabilitation takes place.

Nor must it be assumed that the local authorities can undertake all the rehabilitation alone. All our expertise must be brought in, and that involves voluntary agencies and private builders even though the local authority would be the main agent and moving spirit.

Some of our big private builders are already beginning to see that if they are going to stay in business they must divert some of their resources into rehabilitation, and we should not let this thinking develop piece-meal, but rather create a specific role for private enterprise for the public benefit.

The ultimate aim should be urban coalitions, involving the people living in the area, local authority, private enterprise, voluntary agencies, and backed by highly skilled administration and "banks" of professional skills.

(Readers should look to chapter nine to see what is being done by SHELTER in Liverpool 8.)

Yet again we come back to the leadership: only vigorous leadership can make the exciting possibilities of the 1969 Housing Act a reality. You don't rehabilitate nearly five million homes by sitting in Whitehall and issuing circulars.

7. The Vulnerable

Another harsh reality of the housing problem is that no matter what is done, a small group of people always seem in the end to be missing out. Any system of housing subsidies or allowances must cater more sympathetically for the vulnerable–the larger family, the old, the disabled, fatherless familities, etc. It's not sufficient to give them extra subsidies–they must be given the kind of massive injection of help that will lift them off the floor once and for all. The answer would probably be special incentives to encourage specialist housing associations in each of the fields concerned.

8. Security

Clearly the Rent Act is not yet working satisfactorily and the main flaw is that furnished accommodation does not come under the major security provisions.

Nothing is more likely to antagonise people on the political–right than the suggestion that security should be further extended, and yet the dialogue that often takes place is about two different things: the campaigner for abolition of the difference between furnished and unfurnished housing is nearly always concerned with overcrowded twilight zones, whilst the defenders of the difference are often most concerned about seaside towns, and less heavily populated areas.

The answer, along with so many other aspects of housing, is to make legislation more flexible.

Full security should exist in the twilight zones and inner parts of our bigger cities, where one can no longer overlook the competition and exploitation that still takes place. The argument that this would discourage private landlords does not apply if we rule them out in terms of having a continuing role in the twilight zones anyway.

This, together with an exphasis on tenants' rights propaganda in twilight zone areas, could help enormously to reduce insecurity.

9. Voluntary Housing

There's no doubt that the voluntary housing movement is going to play a significant role in the years to come. Some say it could be providing up to 20% of our housing stock.

In my view the most careful thought should be given to how the special qualities of volunteers are encouraged to flourish, and not allowed to be frustrated.

Central to this would be the creation of a voluntary housing agency, to replace the National Federation of Housing Societies, and possibly the Housing Corporation, to become the national co-ordinator of voluntary activity.

Through it could be diverted all of the money at present loaned through local authorities to housing associations. It could make the money available to housing associations more efficiently without leaving them at the mercy of local authorities who are often over-worked in other respects, and unable to process their applications quickly, or who vary enormously in their attitude to housing associations, according to their political persuasion.

The agency would encourage participation in housing, by helping in the formation of urban coalitions, and pushing housing co-operatives and self-build associations.

It would be entrusted with the provision of incentives to specialist agencies dealing with the most vulnerable in the housing field.

It might be considered that some money for 100% home loans would be allocated to the agency. It would get a share of the money at present going to local authorities (though one would hope this would be massively boosted) to help families in urgent need and unable to get a mortgage on the open market. The agency would then, in turn, make that home loan money available to the best housing aid and advisory centres.

Like some of my other suggestions this is not in itself entirely original. For instance the need for a "housing bank" has been floated for a number of years.

The agency would take over communication in housing, being responsible for publicizing the Rent Act, the House Act 1969, and any other incentives in housing. It would be responsible for the salesmanship of housing bonds.

Finally, it would be responsible for promoting housing aid and advice, sending project teams to all of the priority areas with a brief to set up centres and make them operational as quickly as possible. From a network of about twenty centres, the concept of housing aid and advice would be practiced, developed, and then extended throughout the country.

The role of the housing aid and advisory centres will need to be related to local authority activities, and each centre will need to reflect the services available in its own area.

(More information on housing aid and advice can be found in chapter 9.)

The SHELTER Story

SHELTER, the National Campaign for the Homeless, launched on December 1, 1966, has been an ambulance service and a pressure group.

But, on a small sçale, it has tested many of the thoughts expressed in this chapter–it has shown that there is a ready response to leadership in housing, a readiness to invest in housing if it rids our country of the scandal of the homeless, and an untapped pool of manpower. It has explored the concepts of neighbourhood rehabilitation, housing aid and advice.

Most important, it has set rolling a bandwagon of public concern about housing need that offers the new Minister of Housing a unique opportunity to mobilize the resources he needs to solve the problem, as it can be solved, in the next decade.

SIX THE SHELTER STORY

"We recognise the value and humanity of the work done by the overseas aid charities and the genuine motivation of many of those who contribute to them, but we refuse to accept the salving of consciences. Too often it is the equivalent of tossing sixpence in a beggar's cap: money given by those who have no intention of changing the system that produces beggars and no understanding that they are part of it." *The Haslemere Declaration*

"... faith, hope, charity, these three; but the greatest of these is charity." *1 Corinthians 13:13*

IS CHARITY STILL "THE GREATEST"?

In the mid-1960s there was a growing dissatisfaction in Britian with the politcal system, and the quality of its achievement.

The character of our society had been changing, but the forces and institutions that governed and administered it had not.

As long as the majority were able to convince themselves that they had "never had it so good" it was possible for them to acknowledge this antiquity with a kind of complacent amusement, but when it began to become embarrassing, complacency turned into dissatisfaction and the ruling Party for the past 13 years was pushed out of office. When this, too, did not appear to bring about fundamental change, the national temper became less rational.

The youth of the nation put its changing moods into sharp focus. Firstly, they laughed–satire became the rage, with "That Was The Week That Was" and "Private Eye" to the fore. Then came Harold Wilson, borrowing heavily from the electioneering tactics of John F. Kennedy, and the young people who couldn't vote gave their time to addressing envelopes and pushing leaflets through the door. Those old enough to vote, voted Labour. Again, the older generation that had chuckled indulgently at the satire, gradually followed with their votes, cautiously moving to the left in 1964 by giving Labour a majority of only four, but then massively rejecting the Conservatives in 1966. With the failure of Wilson and the Labour Party to perform miracles overnight, there came a break-up in the solidarity of change. Less than 18 months after the demolition of the Conservatives at the polls in the General Election, Labour was crushed in a landslide swing to the Conservatives in council elections all over the country.

Youth, in the meantime, had largely abandoned party politics, some "dropping out", some–prominent among students–moving to the far-left in political terms, but a surprising number turning to organisations concerned with political issues, but not with party politics.

The arrival of SHELTER in December, 1966, was partly incidental, in that it was bred by a voluntary housing movement that had been there for years. Further, some, though by no means all of its founders were plugged into the existing system, or representative of the middle-class paternalism that had characterised charity in Britain since Victorian days.

But the arrival of SHELTER was also in part symptomatic of its time, both because others of the individuals involved, including myself, were there partly in rebellion against the inadequacy of the party political system, and because it built into its philosophy and its practice a rejection of so much that had become out-dated in the thinking and working of institutionalised charity.

In 1968 a number of young people concerned with the "developing countries met to write "The Haslemere Declaration", from whence came the quotation at the beginning of this chapter. Their pamphlet was significant not just because it slammed Britain's record in overseas aid, but because it confronted charities with a biting criticism of their traditional role. It was as relevant to the poor world that existed within Britain as it was to the poor world without.

> **"We cannot continue to merely be polite, respectable, and ineffective lobbyists for 'more and better aid' when we have lost all faith in the ability of our governments to respond realistically to the desperate human need of the poor world . . . we therefore intend to become involved in a political campaign . . .."**

Behind "The Haslemere Declaration" and the thinking of many others, not least the SHELTER team was belief in at least three principles that presented themselves as essential to voluntary activity in the latter part of the twentieth century:

Firstly, volunteers had to balance two things–they must never under-estimate their own potential, but at the same time they must always keep themselves in perspective, relating their achievement on a limited front with what had to be done by society, through its elected representatives, on the whole front.

Secondly, genuine concern could not be accepted as a passport to involvement on its own, at least not where the real action was to be found. It was not enough to care–one had to be able to get results. Idealism and professionalism had to be linked.

Thirdly, one had to question the value of charity itself. In some instances, it could be a form of oppression. In others, it tackled a symptom of the problem, instead of the cause–economic or social powerlessness. In most, it helped individuals, but only touched the fringes of mass need.

The days when charity in Britain could be caricatured as "the rich giving to help the poor", the lord of the manor opening his gardens to "the people from the village" once a year, and a kind of monster middle-class jumble sale, were over.

To sum up, it was possible for the critics of charities to allege that charities stood in the way of change. Now the aim of many was to put them in the forefront of change.

I've tried to build a sense of perspective, ruthless professionalism, and a belief in participation into every aspect of the work of SHELTER, and it is worth looking at how I've interpreted what I believe to be the demands of our time in such a way that SHELTER could play its part in changing the face of charity in Britain.

Perspective

In naming SHELTER the National *Campaign* for the Homeless, we deliberately set the scene for voluntary activity that went beyond rescue.

Our concern about the homeless, our specialist knowledge of their circumstances and needs, and our involvement in one of the major social problems of our time were ample justification, in our view, for entering into the public-cum-political arena.

It was clear that we were going to become as overwhelmed with the extent of the suffering we would face as overseas aid charities like Oxfam were overwhelmed by the plight of millions of men, women and children in the under-developed countries. Invaluable though our rescue operations were–and they need no defence–they were inadequate. The real, long-term answers to problems of exploitation and inequality lay with the priorities and policies of the politicians. As I said to a SHELTER Rally:

> **"For every family SHELTER can help, it must send nearly one hundred away. As they stumble from its door, unaided, and still homeless, does it forget them? Does it sink into the same sea of complacency based on its own achievements, and become as indifferent to its inadequacies as the politicians seem to be of theirs? In our view the answer is 'no.'**

SHELTER recognised that to combine its rescue operation with political pressure would alienate some of the traditional supporters of charitable work, but took the view that if a charity was to remain silent about the real horror of the situation, or about the inadequacy of official attempts to solve it, it would be guilty of appalling cowardice. Now as never before was a time for courage. The volunteer must speak out with pride about his achievements but with desperation and pity about his failures.

It's all a matter of keeping oneself in perspective. This is not to say that the volunteer can't achieve a lot–he can, and he should never under-estimate his ability to do so. Far too many people avoid getting involved because they believe a problem is too big for them, without recognising that only by doing their bit, along with their neighbour, will it ever be solved. Perspective, in the context of the work of a charity, simply demands that it exists always as a servant of need.

There are two dangers inherent in getting involved in tackling need: the first is that one may give society as a whole the impression that because one is active, one is effective, and though one may well be so on a minor scale, society must always be cognizant of the major problems that remain, and that only society–a fair and just society–can eradicate. Secondly, it's possible that if the volunteer makes inroads into the emergency tip of a problem, he might take sufficient political steam out of the issue to let the authorities off the hook.

The answer to this lies in the charity's own hands: in explaining what it has achieved with the money raised, its emphasis should always be on the problem that remains–a problem it can highlight by speaking out with credibility on a platform of achievement and experience.

This is where many, particularly the young, are so wrong in assessing the value of the volunteer in black-and-white terms. To them, immediate concern leading to immediate action to help the under-privileged is sometimes scorned as a sign of weakness. But a problem like the housing problem deserves an all-out assault. Nothing less will do. Just as in war, one deploys different troops for different purposes. One attacks the oppressors, and the oppressive system. One rescues the fallen or wounded. The tactical problem is one of balance.

In my view the question of whether or not one should offer immediate help is one that just cannot arise. Starving children or homeless families are the immediate challenge to the priorities of campaigns like Oxfam and SHELTER, and their everyday concern for them establishes their value and integrity as long-term campaigns. Urgent human need cannot be ignored for the sake of long-term or other objectives. The under-privileged of today should not be weapons in our political armoury, or irrelevancies in the path of revolutionary change. Intolerance should not be fought with extreme intolerance.

Nor is it just the *movement's* morality that is at stake; the rescue operation itself, often based on such mundane things as money-raising, is also a practical way for *individuals* to express their personal concern and morality, no matter how far they are separated from the front line. Raising the money far from where it will be spent is not the easy way out. It's the toughest part of charity. It's the least popular part. It separates the people who want to jump on any bandwagon to push a variety of political ideas from the people who are prepared to dirty their hands. The value of a campaign based on hard work, and placing heavy responsibility on everybody involved, is that it quickly sheds the talkers.

But, in any event, the rescue operation is not unrelated to the pressure activities, for the knowledge and experience that is essential to tackling the problems comes from grassroots activity.

I often wonder if the "great revolution" came, what the revolutionary Minister of Housing would do. Houses do not spring up overnight. Housing and planning and communications and employment all go together in a gigantic complex, and realistic policies based on experience will alone offer worthwhile achievement.

Because SHELTER is mixed up with bricks and mortar, house purchase and house conversion, management and maintenance, it can hold its own in any dialogue; it not only wants to create change but knows what should be changed.

The combined rescue operation and pressure group not only makes the best and most effective use of the existing system and resources but, at the same time, can experiment where bureaucracy often can't. And experiment is an essential part of pressure. Sometimes the best way to change things is to create an exciting alternative so that people will become disillusioned with the status quo, and point to what the volunteer is doing, and say: "There . . . that is what we want too."

In later chapters I will outline the variety of activity undertaken by SHELTER to rescue homeless families or help them to help themselves, and also the pressure activities, and the reader will get some idea of the balance SHELTER has endeavoured to maintain between the two.

In the meantime, its success can be judged by the comments of leader writers in some of our leading newspapers:

> **"It has rightly been said that SHELTER is the current pioneer in the charity field in the same way as Oxfam was in the late 'fifties'. It indeed represents a new aggressive form of charity, more drawn to protest and stinging attack than to handing round the collecting box. Thanks to SHELTER's scathing publicity, the squalid conditions of the hidden homeless are no longer hidden and the public conscience in this respect is no longer dormant."**
>
> *Leader in the Evening Standard, July 22, 1969.*

You will note that even though SHELTER had been breaking its fundraising target for three years, the "Standard" leader writer saw it as "more drawn to protest and stinging attack". This underlines SHELTER's achievement in maintaining the balance between publicising what it has done, and the problem that remains.

This is perhaps even better seen in what the Guardian leader said on SHELTER'S third birthday, on December 1, 1969:

> **"Rehousing three families a day, as SHELTER is helping to do, makes only a small dent in the numbers of the homeless . . . Yet SHELTER the National Campaign for the Homeless, will deserve all the congratulations it gets on its third birthday today, even though the 2,330 families it has helped so far to a better home represents a distressingly small proportion of the hundreds of thousands which cannot hope to be rescued by charity, but must depend on the scale of the national housing effort. SHELTER knows how to blow a virtuoso fanfare to proclaim its own performance. But its performance**

> **has been not only in fundraising, but in its clear, decisive recognition that a charity of this sort must also get into the political arena, shake up ministries and parties, and help focus public opinion on Government policies. SHELTER's director, Des Wilson, has certainly done that. He has had some blistering rows with politicians, regardless of party— and he has appeared at the Conferences of each of the three Parties. SHELTER has played a necessary part in keeping critical watch on housing policy at a time when less single-minded people might have been taken in by the Ministry of Housing statistical complacency."**

An article in The Observer on January 11, 1970, by Ivan Yates, showed how since the advent of SHELTER and "The Haslemere Declaration" the role of charity had changed dramatically. He said:

> **"Charities used to be anxious to keep out of politics for fear that their fundraising may slacken or dry up. Many are still very careful. One of the four voluntary agencies in famine relief, Save the Children Fund, under world patronage and rather establishment-minded, still tries to keep its nose clean. It refused to join in the current campaign, Action for World Development. The three that did join in, Oxfam, Christian Aid, and War on Want, felt it essential to educate as well as beg; in other words, to educate individuals to give but also to demand similar action of the Government."**

Of SHELTER, Ivan Yates wrote:

> **"SHELTER, which raises nearly a million pounds a year, is even more vulnerable to attack because the**

> **housing shortage is bound to be the stuff of domestic politics. But Des Wilson, its young Director, is adamant that he will not separate the two sides of SHELTER's work. 'If SHELTER has to be the charity which goes to the wall in order to change the role of charities in this country, we will be that charity, "he says."**

Yates ended his story with this point:

> **"If controversy has the effect of drying up the funds, can it be afforded? Or must political opposition come to be accepted? In an open society it should be hoped that people will give even in the teeth of argument and that politicians will be big enough to welcome the work of bodies like SHELTER, even though on one point or another they disagree with it."**

It is not perhaps surprising that the critics of SHELTER's charitable activities usually have no record of directly helping others themselves. They accuse the donor to SHELTER of "salving his conscience" whilst adopting arguments against SHELTER that are often a way of salving their own.

If there is anyone who thinks SHELTER is letting the authorities off the hook, it is not the authorities themselves.

Indeed, the authorities appear to be rebelling against the new breed of volunteer. The volunteer must take some of the blame for this, for just as the official has often come to see the voluntary organisation in terms of stereo-types—either over-idealistic and unrealistic irritants, or do-gooding and highly-inefficient "Lady Bountifuls"—so the volunteer sometimes creates a stereo-type of the official as an insensitive, inhumane, lazy and cynical bureaucrat.

Some of the most effective partnerships are between

officials, who are themselves impatient with the system, and volunteers who find that an enlightened and influential official can open up opportunities that otherwise would not be there.

My experience is that the most bigoted approach to the volunteers is to be found not among the officials but among many local councillors. I never cease to be amazed by the arrogance of some local politicians who seem to see themselves as the Mayor Daley of their particular part of Britain.

It's not original to say that anarchy often comes as a result of authoritarianism, and many radical volunteers are becoming so frustrated that they are being driven from a preparedness to work within the system and are being made into dissidents and revolutionaries almost against their own will.

I well remember going to see the leader of the council in a London Borough with a small deputation to discuss a voluntary contribution, in this case the opening of a "resident centre" providing housing aid, legal advice, and other services in a deprived part of his Borough. This he treated with the utmost suspicion.

As far as he was concerned, if anything was going to be opened in his Borough, it was going to be opened by him and his Council. He reminded me forcibly that he was the elected representative of the people, omitting to mention that the deprived part of the borough had always voted for the opposite party. He also reminded me of his statutory obligation to the area, omitting to mention that the bulk of the people lived in hopelessly overcrowded slums precisely because he and his like had neglected their statutory obligations to the deprived area for so long.

"If a centre is going to be opened, it must be sponsored by the Council, and when it is properly set-up, with a Committee approved by us and a proper constitution, it can be independently run," he said.

"If it's going to be independently run, why not let it evolve from the volunteers and the people themselves?" I asked.

"Nothing will *evolve,* " he replied, thumping the table and earning a nod of approval from his town clerk. If there was to be voluntary activity, he and his colleagues were going to say what it would be and when it should take place. He outlined some of the things he hoped volunteers would volunteer to do, and it became clear that he was a believer in, to quote that horrible phrase, "harnessing the energies" of volunteers to the undertaking of his responsibilities.

He would have done well to read the Seebohm Committee's Report dealing with volunteers. Underlining the role volunteers have played in pioneering social reform, Seebohm said;

> **"We see them playing a major role in developing citizen participation, in revealing new needs, and in exposing shortcomings in the services."**

This aspect of the role of the volunteer–exposing the shortcomings of the system and catching the needy who fall through the gaps–is something that more than one local authority is clearly unenthusiastic about accepting.

One recalls the classic case of the ruthless oppression of what Seebohm called "the critical and pioneer role" of the volunteer when Wandsworth withdrew its grant to the local branch of the National Council for Social Service because it had dared to criticise the local authority.

When I outlined some of these thoughts in one of my weekly columns in "The Guardian" I was staggered by the number of organisations all over the country who wrote to tell me of similar suppression.

The Seebohm Committee was particularly enlightened about the role of the volunteer, and its words should be put on a plaque and hammered on the wall of every Town Hall in the country:

"The day when they could act as vehicles for upper and middle class philanthropy appropriate to the social structure of Victorian Britain is past. Remnants of old practices and attitudes remain in the condescension and special exclusiveness of a few voluntary organisations, and a suspicion and mistrust by some local authorities. On the whole, however, the established voluntary organisations are reviewing and assessing critically their policies and new types of voluntary organisations are emerging, often around "self-help" groups and increasingly characterised by the youthfulness of their members and the radical nature of their criticisms of the existing services. The local authority will need to tolerate and use the criticisms made by voluntary organisations and not expect the partnership to be without conflict. A certain level of mutual criticism may be essential if the needs of consumers are to be met more effectively and they are to be protected from the misuse of bureaucratic and professional power in either kind of organisation."

Professionalism

The days when running charities was the prerogative of retired army officers and the wives of the landed gentry are over. Not that one wishes to be derogatory to either their concern or their effort, but rather to acknowledge that charities have caught up with the twentieth century with a bang.

Many of the accepted attitudes to charity—that their overheads should *automatically* be low, that their advertising should be dignified and restrained, that they should be a vehicle for kindness and not for criticism—have been ignored by the new breed of charity, prepared to spend money to make money, to use the most modern techniques of publicity for those in most need of them, and to speak out almost uncharitably about the neglect they find.

The charity expects to talk to the professional on a professional basis, and indeed often aims to set the pace in terms of quality of service.

Charities like SHELTER, interviewing applicants, begin by asking, "What can you do?" taking the view that without idealism the candidate will never last the distance anyway; but having idealism without professionalism, they will not only fail to last the distance but handicap the rest.

Participation

I believe the SHELTER story is a remarkable one. It has played a significant part in changing the face of charity. It has beaten every money-raising target it set itself. It has pushed housing back to the forefront of public attention and kept it there. And it has rescued substantial numbers of families from slums, and given them their first chance of a decent home.

But though SHELTER has been an advance, it has not yet gone far enough.

For its roots remain in the constituency from where the bulk of the supporters of traditional charities come–the middle classes and the middle class suburbs.

I can't echo the intolerance of the revolutionary left to the middle class, for they would deny the middle class the opportunity of caring at all, or expressing their concern. Organisations like SHELTER should, I believe, always create avenues for the middle class to channel their positive feelings, and not present the middle class with a negative front.

Nevertheless charities, by their nature, put the emphasis on individual need and, while this is beyond criticism as a specific contribution, it cannot be the only contribution if the whole problem is to be solved.

An inherent part of poverty and homelessness is

indignity; if the people at present economically and environmentally oppressed are to be released, it must be because they are not socially oppressed. Social freedom does not always come from being welcomed into the arms of others, but often by being given the opportunity to help oneself.

In this respect, SHELTER can again show remarkable contributions, Indeed, it is in no sense a hand-out operation, for all it does is create the opportunity for the families to pay rent for a decent home. The family aren't getting the home for nothing. Nor does the family ask for it for nothing. But SHELTER through its Neighbourhood Action Project in Liverpool has directly involved the people living in the streets of Liverpool 8 in the rehabilitation of their own district, and through the SHELTER Housing Aid Centre in London has helped a great number of families to buy their own home. In all this, SHELTER has sought the participation of the homeless, and this has been some advance.But still not enough.

I've been practically a lone voice in arguing within our segment of the voluntary housing movement itself that it should boost tenants' participation within housing associations, having them represented on the committees, and involving them in many aspects of their work. This the movement has not yet shown itself willing to do.

I am sorry that SHELTER has not been able to play a more positive part in encouraging tenants' associations, street negotiating groups, and co-operatives.

I believe that one of the challenges that lies ahead for SHELTER is to close the gulf between it and its supporters and the homeless themselves. It is when the homeless can identify with SHELTER as a campaign *for and of them* that SHELTER will have finally changed the face of British charity completely.

As the first Director of SHELTER, and the man who has led the SHELTER team to date, I accept this as justifiable criticism of my record at this time, although it is a criticism I can bear. SHELTER is, after all, only in its fourth year, and the firm base has been established and much achieved. I am not discontented with this record, but would become so if I felt that I was unable, or that SHELTER was unable, to recognise the challenges that remain.

If the homeless come together to fight for their rights, and even to break the traditional voting pattern in the twilight zones by voting for real activists in urban affairs instead of party puppets, and by forming themselves into groups to tackle the problems of rehabilitation of their own communities, and into co-operatives, they must know that organisations like SHELTER are there to serve them, even if the best way to do it is to close down.

Among some of the Squatters who appeared in 1969, some of the strikers against higher rents in a situation where rent rebates were inadequate, and among some of the people of Liverpool 8, one can see the genesis of a real movement.

Participation and involvement became the current vogue words in 1969 and '70 and, insomuch as they mean that people should get as much say as they want in the creation and improvement of their immediate surroundings, and of the country that they live in,that's good. But it is an excess of idealism to pretend that participation can come about without leadership, or that where a group of people has been economically and socially oppressed–as some have–and are so obviously a minority in an affluent society , that they can lift hemselves out of the situation and create their own movement. This is not to say that it has not happened before–obviously it has. But in the situations that exist in our twilight zones, it is a less likely possibility.

For this reason, I believe organisations like SHELTER backed by the generosity of the traditional charity-donors, encouraged by enlightened authorities, can play a key role in providing the professionalism and expertise to the people who need them most. Their aim should be to align themselves with the homeless or the poor, or the sufferers of whatever problem is involved, not out of charity but out of a desire to share in the creation of change.

The trouble with charity in Britain in 1970 is that, whereas the word at one time meant an attitude of good will and love for one's fellow man, it has come to mean bureaucratic, class-conscious caring. It's up to SHELTER and the new breed of charities to change all that.

BLACK SPOT: GLASGOW

50,000 families on Council waiting list; 100,000 unfit houses; 70,000 households without hot water; 180,000 people overcrowded

BLACK SPOT: BIRMINGHAM

[illegible] families on waiting list; 50,000 people overcrowded;

BLACK SPOT: LONDON

190,000 families on waiting list; 100,000 unfit houses

BLACK SPOT: LIVERPOOL

70,000 unfit houses; 40,000 households without hot water

35,000 people overcrowded

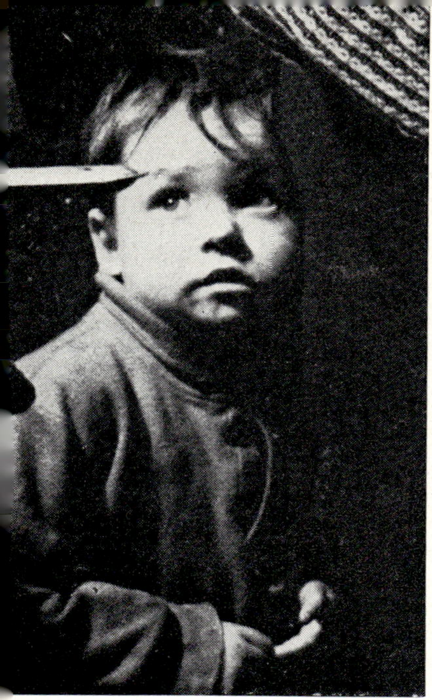
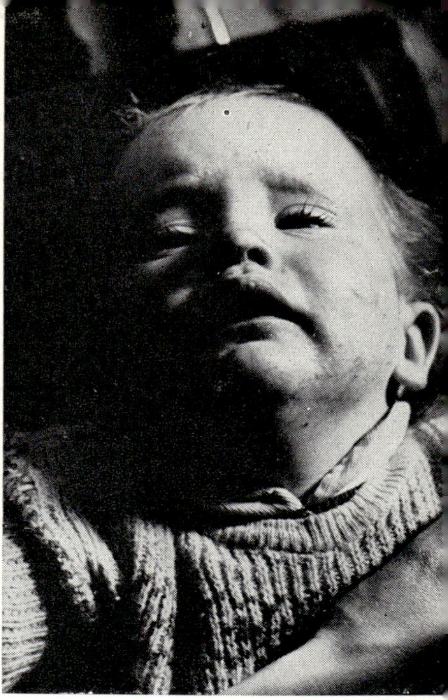
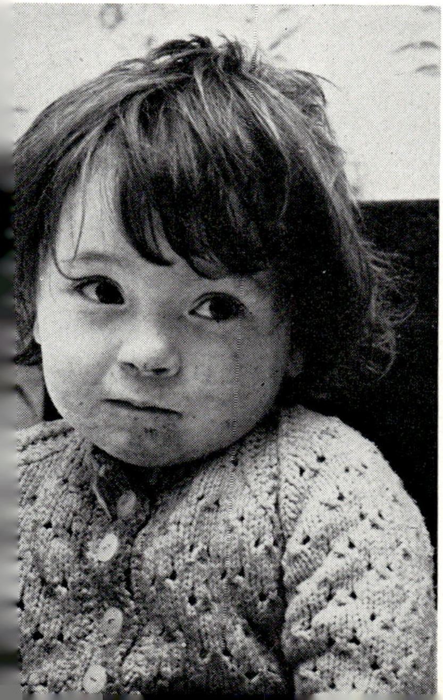

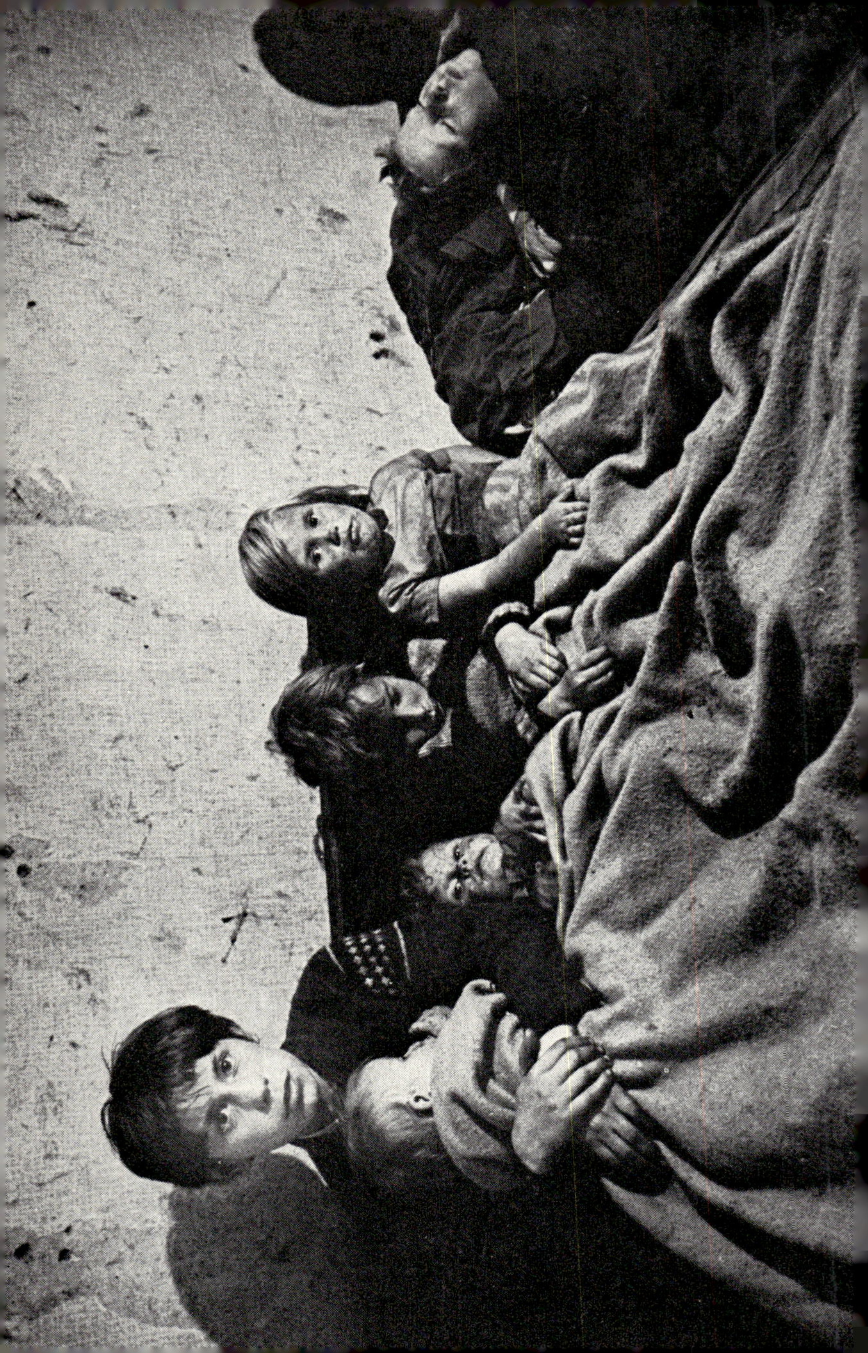

SHELTER Rally, London, 1970

"Face the Facts" Rally, Trafalgar Square, 1969

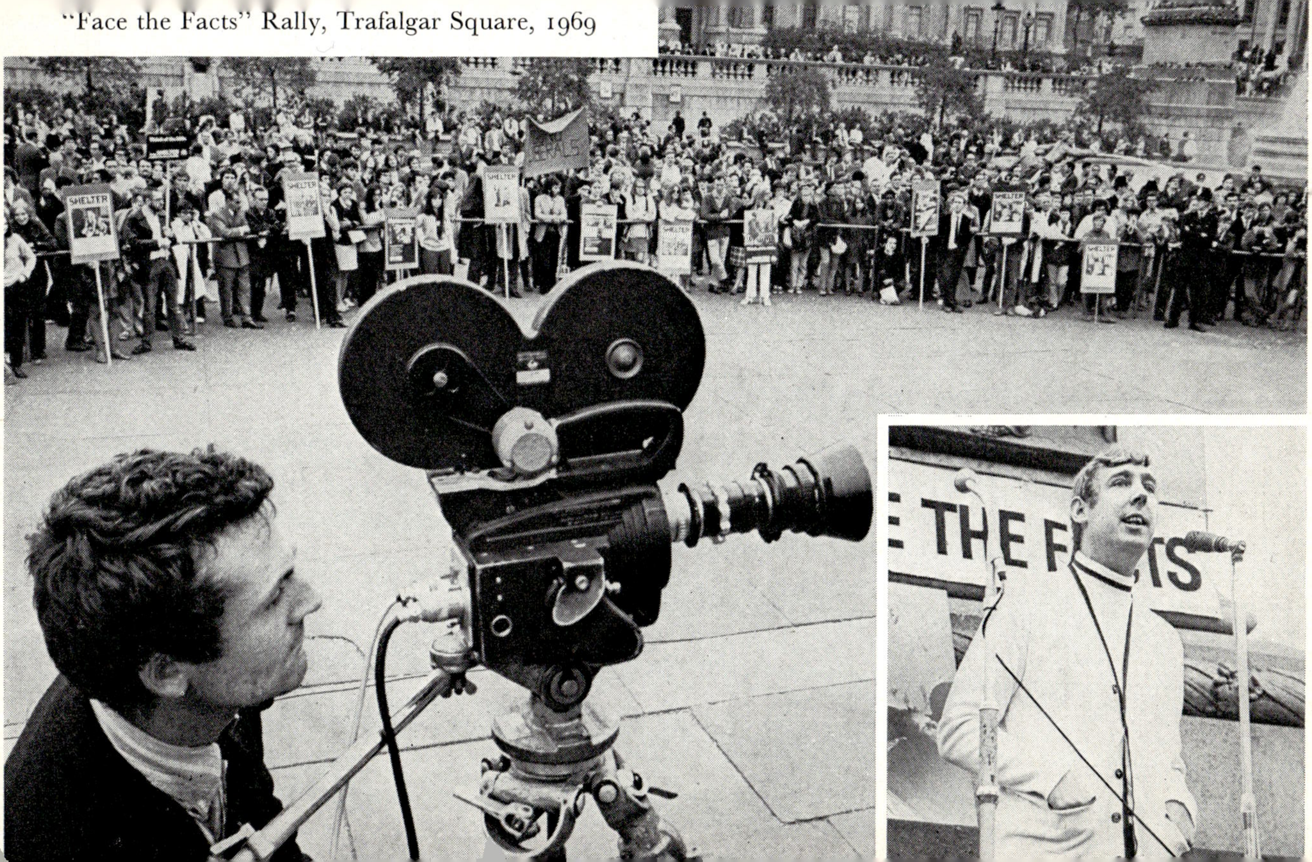

The famous "Christmas – You Can Stuff It" advert

Part of the "Face the Facts" advertising campaign

BRITAIN, THE PROMISED LAND.

1918 Lloyd George promises homes "fit for the heroes who have won the war."
1933 Ministry of Health promises to clear "all areas that require clearance not later than 1938."
1946 Aneurin Bevan: "I give you this promise; that by the next general election there will be no housing shortage as far as the mass of the British people are concerned."
1950 Lord Woolton boasts "We have done more difficult things than rehouse this nation."
1961 Housing White Paper promises "With the exception of a few areas, unfit housing should have practically disappeared within the next ten years."
1965 Ministry of Housing states: "In Great Britain some three million families still live either in slums, near slums or in grossly overcrowded conditions . . ."
1967 Anthony Greenwood admits "About 1.8 million dwellings are unfit (for human habitation). Another 4.7 million are unsatisfactory . . ."

Promises, promises, promises.

That's all the homeless will ever get until society faces this fact: housing is not the personal problem of a few. It's a national crisis.

Send a donation to SHELTER and we promise you this: we'll continue to rescue thousands of desperate families. And we'll keep the pressure on society and its authorities to face the housing facts.

That's a promise that will be kept.

PHOTOGRAPH: PATRICK WARD

SHELTER FACE THE FACTS

National Campaign for the Homeless

86 Strand, London W.C.2.

Two determined Wilso
the former Prime Minist
and the Director of **SHE**
TER at the opening of son
Birmingham Housing Tru
flats

Eamonn Casey, now Bish
of Kerry, who was for tw
years Chairman of **SHE**
TER and a driving force
the whole voluntary housi
movement

Worth Annexe
Pound Hill Co. Jnr. Sch
Church Road,
Crawley,
Sussex
25th Nov 1968

Dear Mr Des Wilson,
I have heard about
Shelter and I think it is a very good idea.
Our School pupils are doing many thing's
to raise money like, puting on a School
concert and having a collection. I feel
very sorry for the homeless and I would
like very much to help because the
children in the home probebly feel
very unhappy. It's all right for the
children that have homes because they
have parents and brothers and sisters
to love them. I am not saying the
children at the home don't get any
love because they do. It's Just that it
is'nt the same kind of love.

Yours Sincerely
Sally Hoskin.

Cindy Barlow

Eileen Ware

John Willis

Ken Willson

Liz Wills

Joan Ruddock

Liz Doyle

Ron Dick

Above: Youth activities raise a quarter of **SHELTER's** million pounds a year

Below: One of the happy families rehoused by **SHELTER's** campaign

SEVEN

"Outside a Kennedy Presidential bid I've never seen dedication and professionalism to equal it."

Anthony Howard, on SHELTER, New Statesman, September, 1969.

ANATOMY OF A CAMPAIGN

The seventh-floor offices in the Strand occupied by the bulk of the SHELTER team had been empty for years and when we moved in, the walls were black with years of accumulated dust. At that time, in June, 1967, there were a dozen of us, but now there are 60-odd people working at 86 Strand.

My office in the corner of the building overlooks the roof-tops linking the Strand with Covent Garden, and its view of the West End is dominated by Centrepoint, the huge office block that has been unoccupied since it was built in 1966, and now stands as a monument to the system that has allowed vast fortunes to be made out of property speculation in London.

It is in my office that Trustees Meetings, and departmental heads' meetings are held.

SHELTER may not like the word "charity" as it is commonly understood, but if the money it raises is not to be subjected to crippling taxes, it has to be registered as a charity, and comply with the conditions essential to this status. In fact, charitable status is not the straitjacket that many people seem to assume, for the Charity Commissioners, who create the necessary safeguards for the public (who are, after all, donating well over £50,000,000 a year to charity), appear to be more enlightened about the need for change in the concept of organised charity than many charities themselves.

The Trustees of SHELTER represent the Charity Commissioners and the public as custodians of the money raised by the charity. They meet three or four times a year, to examine the finances of the charity, and to take broad policy decisions on the allocation of the money under different headings—administration, fund raising, education, housing, housing aid and advice, experimental activity, etc.—and to receive reports from the full time team.

The bulk of SHELTER's money is applied for by local housing groups, and a number of sub-committees, comprising members of the Trustees, the SHELTER team and co-opted experts, meet to discuss the applications in detail.

But, on the whole, SHELTER is notable for its lack of committees, and the free hand given to its Director, and its full-time team

The advantages are clear: the morale of the full-time team is high, because it knows that it controls its own destiny. It's able to work to a clear-cut budget and programme, agreed by the Trustees, but because of the delegation of authority, there is room for plenty of flexibility and quick decision-making. The SHELTER team is itself close to the SHELTER movement in the country, and able to adapt quickly to its moods and views.

Few charities are as dependent on their full-time team as SHELTER, and the selection of its members is taken seriously. Often a candidate will see three or four departmental heads, and emerge after interviews with many other contenders before reaching the short-list state. I've always tried to involve myself fully in the selection of any key member, striving always to find somebody who combines three essential qualities: proven idealism, professionalism, and compatability with the spirit of the SHELTER team.

Unless the candidates really care, there is little possibility that they will withstand the pressure of work at SHELTER, or be prepared to make the sacrifices, both in terms of income and loss of spare time, that working at headquarters involves. But that idealism is only the beginning. They must be able to show that they are not only professionally equipped to do the work, but outstandingly so. They will be working among people who not only set themselves high standards, but whose time is at a premium, and who can't afford to be let down by their colleagues and are intolerant of anything less than near-perfection from the people and services with whom they work.

Finally they've got to be able to "fit in". The emphasis is on self-discipline. Although we're fairly firm about basic office hours, the main criterion is that people do well what they are there to do. They dress as they like, comforted by the thought that their Director is often mistaken for a window cleaner by strangers to the organisation. Jeans and jumpers are worn by both the sexes, although the mini-skirts of some of the SHELTER girls are the envy of Fleet Street. Everybody is known by their Christian name and a visitor can never tell who are the departmental heads and who are not. The offices are overcrowded, the telephones never stop ringing and even the typewriter clatter has an intensity all of its own.

Occasionally someone comes to the SHELTER team assuming all this informality adds up to relaxation. They don't last long. They soon find the pace is set by the person at the next desk, and that behind the casual surface lies a spirit of dedication and self-discipline that gets far better results than dictatorship from above ever could.

If you were to look at a chart showing the departmental breakdown of SHELTER, you would see the Director's office as a central dynamo, rather than a dictator of the pace.

The Director's office is regarded as a department in its own right, no only being responsible for maintaining overall direction and liaison, but also for certain chores, like the organisation of major conferences, the preparation of the SHELTER newspaper and some aspects of public relations.

Much of the tying-up of ends takes place at meetings of the "Liaison Committee", the group of ten departmental heads and myself.

This group is responsible for devising the campaign plan for the year. On a weekend in the Autumn the departmental heads, together with regional organisers, disappear into the country to discuss all aspects of SHELTER policy and draw up an outline of what the campaign will seek to achieve in the following year. From this, the Liaision Committee creates its campaign plan, fixes a target (in 1970, a million pounds) and works out the activities that will need to be undertaken to achieve that result.

The activities are spread over the year in such a way that the organisation is not over-taxed at any one point, and each departmental head takes responsibility for one or more of the activities. Some, such as the Public Relations Director, are responsible for servicing all of the activities, from the Youth Campaign to, as was the case in 1969, the Round Britain Walk.

The Liaison Committee meetings vary, according to the temperature of the campaign, often being businesslike and cool, but occasionally developing into fierce argument.

Because SHELTER is a young organisation, most of its departmental heads are the only people to have held their particular position. Many of them had little experience when they came to SHELTER, but from being thrown in at the deep end have become highly experienced. They haven't survived, and made a success of their work, by being introverted, and both the speed and standard of debate at Liaison Committee meetings are high.

A feature of the SHELTER team is the combination of youth and experience. I doubt whether any charity of comparable size has such a mixture at its top decision-making level. Thus two departmental heads are around the 50 mark, three in their thirties, and the remainder in their twenties. Once past departmental heads, the SHELTER team is even younger, several members being in their teens, and the majority in their early twenties.

On the whole, applicants for positions at SHELTER tend to be between 21 and 24, many of them looking for somewhere to go directly from university.

Perhaps significant is that for all their idealism, the majority haven't been involved in party politics, and see SHELTER as an alternative way of "getting involved". Others have played at the fringes of party politics, and become disillusioned.

On the whole, they tend to be doers rather than talkers.

The pressure within the organisation tends to shift according to what activity is being undertaken at any particular time.

Thus, for nearly three months while the youth campaign was at its height in 1968 Eileen Ware, our Youth Director, was working around 90 hours a week.

Salary levels are low. Because secretaries are the hardest to recruit, one has to pay near to the market rate, and this means that there is little difference between the highest and the lowest salaries. There's no doubt that if the salary scales at SHELTER were lifted to meet the ability and market value of the people there, the salary bill would be practically doubled.

SHELTER's departmental heads are:

Appeal Co-ordinator: Ken Willson, who at 50 is one of

the older members of the team. Well-known in the sporting world, he was for four years Chief Administrator for the World Cup Series in Britain, and we managed to capture him shortly afterwards. Ken came in to co-ordinate our fund-raising activity, and quickly established himself as a popular and fantastically hardworking member of the team. His background may not be one of youthful idealism, but when it comes to commitment to the SHELTER cause he is surpassed by no one. He is responsible for linking together all of the appeals activities, providing the print material, and controlling the budgets.

Public Relations Director: Liz Wills was 23 when she came to SHELTER from the National Council of Social Service, where she had been an Information Assistant. When she was Groups Director she travelled round the country at such speed she became known as "Whiz Liz". She is a first class administrator, speaker and writer, but her outstanding characteristic is an ability to bounce back from any setback, and to burn up any momentary fury or frustration in one mighty explosion. Thus she's capable of storming out of one's office, slamming the door so that the crockery rattles, then bouncing in two or three moments later in high good humour, oblivious to what had gone before. The strength of the SHELTER movement in the country owes a lot to her energy and enthusiasm, and now she co-ordinates all SHELTER exhibitions, speaking engagements, photography, and publicity with the same drive.

Youth Director: Eileen Ware was 23 when she came to SHELTER, and had been a newspaper reporter. She had been keenly involved in youth affairs, having written a pamphlet on Rights at 18, and been a member of the Young Liberals and the British Youth Council. Even by SHELTER's standards, she is tremendously hardworking, undertaking speaking tours that would daunt the toughest of politicians. She once gave 22 talks in three days. Eileen is tall and blonde, and wears mini-skirts that are a sensation in the boys' schools that she visits. Her achievement as Youth Director of SHELTER has pushed her into the forefront of Britain's youth organisers, and she and her small team of girls in the youth office have raised well over half a million pounds.

Groups Director: Joan Ruddock was 24 when she came to the SHELTER team as a Regional Organiser in the Home Counties, and in 1969 she took over from Liz as Groups Director. Outwardly calm and quiet-spoken, Joan is tougher and more ambitious than she looks, and an extremely able administrator. She is responsible for creating SHELTER Groups, co-ordinating their work throughout the country, and leads the biggest departmental team—10 regional organisers, and their secretaries.

Appeals Organiser: George Nicholson is known as the team's "Resident Tory". George was to fight Bob Mellish in Bermondsey at the General Election and has to put up with the persistent teasing of other members of the SHELTER team. George refuses to concede that he is any less radical, however, and is a forceful and capable Appeals Organiser, who has done much to establish SHELTER among churches, as well as being responsible for SHELTER's advertising campaign.

Special Events Organiser: Liz Doyle also came to SHELTER as a Regional Organiser, but after touring the East Anglian Groups for a year, became SHELTER's first Special Events Organiser at the age of 21. Although the youngest departmental head, she has strong views on how she should raise the £100,000 expected from her and is proving too good to invite much contradiction. Her infectious enthusiasm makes her ideal for organising grassroots activity.

The above departmental heads are responsible for raising the bulk of the money in England and Wales, and they are backed by young, long-suffering Regional Organisers, operating either from SHELTER Headquarters in London, or from small branch offices in Manchester and Birmingham.

Liz Wills is backed up by a talented young Press Officer, Richard Plumridge, who joined us in June, 1969, photographer, Nick Hedges, who has taken most of the photographs used in SHELTER publicity, and designer, Ian Mattingley.

It says much for the standard of the second-level executives, that it is now rarely necessary to recruit people for top positions from outside the organisation.

It is notable that none of the above had undertaken similar work before they came to SHELTER.

SHELTER in Scotland has a structure similar to the main headquarters, with a Director responsible to myself in London, and then its own Groups and Youth Organisers, and its own Administration.

Ronald Dick, our Scottish Director, comes down to Liaison Committee Meetings, and has achieved remarkable success since the Scottish office was opened in October, 1968.

The expenditure of SHELTER money is concentrated around three departmental heads–our Housing Director, John Willis; our Housing Co-ordinator, Cindy Barlow; and Research and Information Director, Miles Davies.

John Willis was Rent Officer in Oxford before becoming Secretary of the Housing Societies Charitable Trust, an organisation that was responsible for the distribution of some of SHELTER's money. So impressed were we with John that we invited him to come on to the SHELTER team as Housing Director. One of the SHELTER team who still prefers to wear a suit, John nevertheless thrives on the informality, and is highly popular among the younger members of the team. His responsibilities are considerable–investigating the effectiveness of housing associations applying for or using SHELTER money, advising them on how to make the most effective use of the money, investigating opportunities for spreading the work of SHELTER to other parts of the country, and negotiating with national and local authorities to enable SHELTER money to be multiplied with as much statutory help as possible. In addition, he supervises the expenditure of SHELTER money on special area projects. John gives way on idealism to no one, but his feet are firmly rooted among the harsh realities of housing economics, and he has added enormously to the stature of the SHELTER team. One envisages him playing an even more significant role in SHELTER as its contribution to the housing policy grows.

Cindy Barlow is Secretary to the Trust, and possibly the youngest Secretary of a major charity in the country. She came to SHELTER in 1967 when she was 23 and was administrator of the campaign until, in addition to her responsibilities as Secretary, she became Housing Coordinator. Like John Willis, she is a Trustee of the SHELTER Housing Aid Centre in London, the SHELTER Neighbourhood Action Project in Liverpool, and the SHELTER Housing and Renewal Experiment in Bradford, and in addition to co-ordinating all of the housing projects, is responsible for the expansion of housing aid and advice. She is specially concerned with promoting the welfare aspects of housing associations. For her age, she is a remarkably firm negotiator, and is one of the most intensely idealistic of the SHELTER team.

Miles Davies, who came to the SHELTER team in 1970, is responsible for running the Information Library, and supervising all research activity. In this capacity, he not only has to keep members of the SHELTER team up to date with what's happening in housing, but also to serve the media, newspapers, radio, and television.

Finally, the organisation is administered by Mary Gill who, as Administrative Director, has the most unenviable of tasks in any campaign organisation.

The effectiveness of this team can be seen by comparing its achievements with its targets over the first three years of operation:

Fundraising

Year	*Target*	*Achieved*
66-68	£270,000 *(min)*	£373,000
68-69	£550,000 *(min)*	£704,000
69-70	£800,000 *(min)*	£1,024,000

Overheads

66-68	25% *(max)*	19%
68-69	20% *(max)*	16%
69-70	20% *(max)*	14%

SHELTER supporters tend to fall into three groups: those who give money regularly, but haven't the time to get further involved; those who do get involved, mainly in SHELTER Groups; and young people, who take part in the Youth Campaign.

SHELTER does not have members, in the sense that there is no subscription, no membership card, and no list of members.

I'm often told that SHELTER is undemocratic, and on paper it is. Its Trustees and its Director are not elected, and there is no opportunity for supporters to influence the policies of SHELTER through a formal structure. But, on the other hand, a movement as loosely defined, and as dependent on its supporters, as SHELTER, has to be run by people who are acutely sensitive all the time to the views of its supporters. Because there is no subscription system, it's no trouble for a supporter to withdraw if he or she is dissatisfied, and thus the pressure on headquarters to be acutely conscious of the need to carry the movement with it, both by making available as much information as possible and by consulting its supporters about main activities in advance, is clear. At the last resort, SHELTER can only beg and request its supporters for help–it cannot demand that help. On many occasions the SHELTER team has gone to its supporters requesting assistance at a certain time of the year, or for a certain fundraising concept, and has been rejected if its supporters don't like the idea.

Thus, the SHELTER team has learned that there is little sense in sitting at 86 Strand and taking decisions about what the movement is going to do. The most it can do is decide what it would *like* to happen, and then go out and discuss it with supporters, usually coming back with a compromise that is the most likely to work, because it is based on a combination of the experience of Headquarters and the grassroots knowledge of its supporters.

I am satisfied that the balance between firm direction, in order to maximise the speed of action and obtain the utmost efficiency, and democracy, in terms of the sharing of views before decision-making, has been kept in SHELTER. I am consoled, too, by the knowledge that some movements that look democratic on paper offer the least opportunities for participation and decision-making in practice.

SHELTER Groups vary enormously and tend to reflect their originators. Thus, if a SHELTER Group has been started by a clergyman, it is often centred round the local church or congregation. But SHELTER Groups are run by housewives, schoolteachers, and people who vary both in the work they do, and in their age group.

A SHELTER Group is a kind of mini-SHELTER–raising money and publicising the plight of the homeless in its own locality.

At the time of writing there are 261 Groups in England

and Wales, and a further 45 in Scotland.

On the whole, members of SHELTER Groups tend to be more militant than the traditional charity supporter, but less doctrinaire than the supporters of political parties. We've found them remarkably understanding of the balance we need to keep between pressure and the more conventional charity operation. At times when SHELTER has been the centre of controversy, they have been encouragingly philosophical, not unquestioning of what SHELTER Headquarters is doing, but content to wait for an explanation or an opportunity to discuss the matter with their Regional Organiser, or somebody else from SHELTER, before passing judgment. It is easy to take this kind of backing for granted, but it wouldn't be possible to be so effective at SHELTER Headquarters if things were different.

Undoubtedly these people, and the bulk of the people on SHELTER's mailing list–people who donate to the campaign–come from the traditional recruiting ground of charities–the middle class, but it's impossible to categorise the young people who've involved themselves in the campaign to such an extent that SHELTER has often been described as a youth movement.

Much of the enthusiasm for SHELTER among our young people can be traced back to a rejection of the political system, and in particular a wish to get more directly involved in tackling problems like housing. I think, too, that young people have been attracted by the youth of the SHELTER team, and by the radical image that extends beyond its pressure activities even into fund-raising.

Every generation of young people has had its central concern. At the time when I came to Britain at the beginning of 1960 it was nuclear disarmanent. For this generation it is poverty–the battle against what has become known as 'The Third World". You don't need to leave the shores of Britain to find that world.

We've tried to make our involvement with youth a two-way thing–whilst we've welcomed their energy and idealism, and their uncorrupted commitment, and all the money they have raised and the publicity they have got, we have, too, tried to spread our knowledge about the problem to them, hoping that as a result of our educational activity they can avoid the pitfalls in the housing jungle and the danger of becoming the homeless of tomorrow.

Some of the sharpest questions that SHELTER speakers are asked come from young people, and their vigilance is a form of protection against complacency within the campaign.

Young people don't go much for talking these days, and you won't see them at SHELTER's conferences or rallies. But they are often a source of inspiration to the Headquarters team, not least because of their sensitivity to the need of others.

This is reflected in some of the poems written by schoolchildren and sent to Eileen Ware.

For instance, this one by 16-years-old Christine Newton, from Scarborough Girls High School:

Homelessness

Outside the lighted window, under the glowing sign
"Frying Tonight", a torn and greasy sheet of paper,
Trampled dirty, blown by the damp polluted city wind
Drifts aimlessly down the street, breaking the surface of puddles
Reflecting the pallid haloes of the city lights.
Homelessness. Do you know what that word means?
I don't. I can only guess that it means a life
Like that piece of paper, drifting, never staying long
In one place. Always moving on, with no rest or calm;
No home, no fireside, nothing to call one's own, no pride:

Above all no peace of mind, nothing but fear
For tomorrow, Homelessness is an endless road.
Wet, limp and battered, the paper blows on down the street.

Then, 18-years-old Jennifer Hewitt wrote this; at Bar Convent in York:

I have a room of my own at home:
–a warm room, thick carpeting, bright walls,
curtains, blankets and a comfortable bed.
Yet today I met a girl: a girl poorer than myself,
(I thought I was poor because I couldn't buy that latest L.P.)
This girl was poor, miserably poor–
and so were the rest of her family.
Her home is one room–but not like mine.
Hers is a basement–it's dark–
and damp–too damp for the paper to stick on the walls
–even the plaster is flaking off.
There isn't a carpet on the floor. The floor creaks.
Her room is smaller than mine
but there are two beds–double beds.
Here are seven people sharing everything–
I don't share my room with anyone.
It is still as it was this morning–
nothing in it has changed–except me
I have seen
What homelessness can mean.
There isn't a carpet on the floor. The floor creaks.
Here room is smaller than mine
but there are two beds–double beds.
Here are seven people sharing everything–
I don't share my room with anyone.

It is still as it was this morning–
nothing in it has changed–except me
I have seen
What homlessness can mean.

Alison Moorhouse, of Black County Primary School, Lancashire, who is only ten years old, wrote this:

There are people, who live in this country
Who have no homes at all
The children who belong to these familys
Are little weak and small

There are some people who help them
But there are not enough
To save some starving people
In clothes so ugly and rough

But sometime things will be better
And there wont be as many as now
Of these poor, poor people
But how will we save them How?

From the word "go" the emphasis in SHELTER was on publicity. When you are launching a major charity with no nation-wide movement, little knowledge of the problem you are tackling, and the need for quick results before your money runs out, you are totally dependent on getting the campaign before the public, and keeping it there.

This emphasis on publicity undoubtedly paid off, for although SHELTER is still raising less than many other charities, it probably ranks with Oxfam as the best known.

I've not hesitated to allow myself to be pushed forward as a public personality, and although this has been a matter of some criticism, I have had the enthusiastic backing of most of my colleagues. The motive is simple–we live in an age of personalities, dominated by personality-type radio and television programmes, and newspaper columns, and through the projection of an individual, SHELTER was able to project itself, and thus the problem of the homeless, to vast audiences.

No other campaign has had the television coverage that has been achieved by SHELTER and it is fair to say that two-thirds of the opportunities were only there because we had a personality to fit the bill.

I've been well aware of the criticism of SHELTER's preparedness to indulge in the "personality cult", but as far as I've been concerned there is only one question to ask: "Does it help SHELTER to have a personality at its head?" You only have to look at the list of radio and television appearances and the newspaper articles, and the opportunities used for SHELTER, and indeed the place SHELTER has in public recognition, to see that the answer is "yes".

One of the techniques that proved highly effective in the days when we were establishing SHELTER in the provinces was what I called "barn storming" after the American electioneering approach.

We would choose a town and organise a public meeting. Then I would "hit town" in the late afternoon, recording a television appearance on the commercial channel, and then appear live on B.B.C. Often this led to me appearing on both local T.V. news programmes at the same time. From there I would go to the local radio news programme and between then and the public meeting often give interviews to two or three newspapers. The following morning I would speak to the biggest school in town. By the time I had left, less than twenty hours after arriving, we would have notched up about as much exposure as it was possible to get in that town at that time.

My own day begins at 8.30, when I arrive at 86 The Strand, at about the same time as the post gets there. The majority of the SHELTER team get in between 9 and 9.30 and I count on this intervening hour to deal with correspondence before telephones begin to ring, and the action really begins.

My post bag contains everything, from a handful of stamps saved up by an old age pensioner and a moving little note, to a letter from the Minister of Housing. There are requests to speak, and to write articles, usually balanced by letters of complaint about something I have written or said in the previous week. There is nearly always at least one application to work at SHELTER, and there are usually several desperate letters from homeless families.

I usually have at least one press release, article, or speech to write every day, and I try to do this first thing in the morning as well.

In addition to the Liaison Committee, that usually meets on a Monday morning, there could be a meeting with John, Cindy and Miles to talk about the distribution of SHELTER money, or a meeting of Ken Wilson's fund-raising committee. On the first Monday of each month all the Regional Organisers come in for a meeting and exchange of experiences. The meetings usually take place in the morning. Lunch is often taken with a journalist, or I go without, so that I can write an article or a speech in the office. I try to fix most of my individual appointments in the afternoon, for I have discovered that the best time for desk work is in the morning or late afternoon and that mid-afternoon is most profitably spent in conversation. Often one is rushing off in the evening to speak anywhere within one hundred miles of London.

Not that there is an average day in SHELTER, for one spends a lot of time travelling around, both to take part in meetings about expenditure of SHELTER money, and to speak at conferences and to raise money for the homeless.

Radio and television programmes also take one out of the office a great deal.

On the first Monday of each month the SHELTER team gathers in the evening so that departmental heads and I can brief the full team on various activities taking place, and so that the Director of one of our housing projects can come along, give a talk and answer questions. If any member of the SHELTER team is leaving, then this also becomes a farewell "do".

As I look at SHELTER as it now is, I get a tremendous sense of satisfaction that I have created the kind of organisation that I, if I were not Director, would like to work for: in which people can be individuals, and yet essentially a team; in which discipline is self-imposed, because that is the way team members want it; in which there are no formal coffee-breaks, ways of dressing, or ways of addressing seniors; indeed, in which there are no seniors; in which there is much self-criticism but even more loyalty; in which the excitement of today helps to heal the wounds, no matter how deep, of yesterday's battle.

I like to think, too, that the SHELTER team reflects its time–young people committed to standards of human behaviour not based on hypocritical socially-imposed morality but on generosity and respect of other human beings. They laugh, love, drink, smoke, and dress like the res–throwing themselves into the 1970 way of life, and even more so, but putting far more back in than they ever take away.

They lift two articulate fingers to cant, don't patronise, and express their care through action. In an extraordinary way they exert their remarkable personalities whilst at the same time being self-effacing in SHELTER's service.

In the anatomy of SHELTER they are the heart, pumping love and energy to all of the movement, and life blood into its work.

They were all significant individuals long before I came along. But as a team they *are* my creation and my pride in them knows no bounds.

EIGHT

December 1, 1966

"SHELTER, National Campaign for the Homeless, launched at a press conference in the Crypt of St. Martin-in-the-Fields, London, today, brings five major national bodies in the voluntary housing association movement together to publicise the emergency situation that exists within the housing problem, and appeal for money to carry out a rescue operation for homeless families in the "blackspot" cities of London, Birmingham, Liverpool and Glasgow."

SHELTER Press Release.

THE SHELTER STORY (1): TARGET—ONE MILLION POUNDS A YEAR

On top of a filing cabinet in Liz Wills' publicity office are three massive book-files containing copies of the 300-odd press releases issued by SHELTER in its first three and a half years. They tell a fascinating story of the birth and growth of a campaign. Between their lines I can see and recall battles won and lost, moments of excitement and exhaustion, days when one was light-headed with success and nights when one's spirit was practically gnawed away with an all-consuming weariness but most of all the closeness and comradeship of the top members of the SHELTER team as we all paid the same price and reaped the same reward while the press releases piled on top of each other, from number one to 300.

From all the news stories, I've extracted about 50 that between them reflect the high spots and the unusual features of SHELTER's campaign. They will lead me into the stories I tell in this chapter and the two that follow.

The SHELTER story is, in fact, the story of three campaigns–to raise the money, to spend the money effectively, and to pressurize society to solve the problem. I've broken the press releases under the three headings, and devoted a chapter to each.

The press release quoted above tells of the launching of SHELTER on December 1, 1966. Behind it lay a year of planning and preparation. The steering committee had represented the National Federation of Housing Societies, British Churches Housing Trust, Christian Action, Catholic Housing Aid Society, and Notting Hill Housing Trust, five organisations that had with varying degrees of success been attempting to raise money for voluntary housing associations.

No one man, least of all myself, founded SHELTER. Indeed, without any one of five men, it is probable that SHELTER might have failed to get off the ground. It's always been a team effort, dependent on a variety of different talents and temperaments.

Initially, the intention was that SHELTER should be responsible for raising the money, and the distribution of it would be undertaken by a sub-committee of the National Federation of Housing Societies. But the raising of money, while essential to all its activities, quickly became the beginning and not the end of SHELTER's responsibilities. Not only did SHELTER take control of all of its distribution of funds but it began to direct much of the voluntary housing operation in such a way that it became the most influential force in the movement, and the most effective negotiator with the authorities. At the same time, it expanded its pressure activities across a wide front.

But all this was a long way ahead when SHELTER was

launched. At that time, the raising of the money so that housing associations could save the most desperate families from overcrowded and squalid conditions was the main concern of SHELTER.

It is no coincidence that the words "rescue operation" and "emergency" figure in the opening paragraphs of the press relaease issued on December 1. Part of the strategy was concentration on a few words and phrases. The emphasis on the "rescue operation in a national emergency" was to overcome the argument that "surely it's the Government's job?". To beat this, we had to convince people that the housing problem was totally out of control and only an all-out effort from everybody could save thousands of families from disaster. Every bit of literature urged "in an emergency we all unite". As I pointed out to the Trustees, "We don't need to invent an emergency–it's there."

The "emergency" technique was adopted, also, to overcome the automatic reaction of the majority that people could only become homeless because of their own inadequacies. "In an emergency situation like this there have to be innocent victims" our material said.

We set out to beat the anti-large family set by focusing our appeal for sympathy on the helplessness of children–"It's not *their* fault a generation of children grown up in misery. Will you help now?".

Among the catch-phrases chosen, the term "hidden homeless" was to figure largely, and the statistic we chose to drum home again and again was taken from the 1965 White Paper–" 3 million families in Britain today still live either in slums, near slums, or grossly overcrowded conditions".

Britain was going through a freeze and a squeeze, and launching a fresh fundraising organisation was not going to be easy, so it was decided to add to the impact by launching SHELTER at Christmas, both to take advantage of the goodwill that undoubtedly exists at that time, and to contrast the family life of the majority with the misery of the slum dweller.

A press conference was called in the Crypt of St. Martin-in-the-Fields in London and receptions organised for Birmingham, Liverpool, and Glasgow in the following week.

The Trustees, who were meeting frequently, had appointed me as Campaign Director, and with little money and no background to the Campaign, I decided to closely integrate advertising, direct mail, and public relations so that we could cover as much ground as possible at the minimum cost. Every newspaper, magazine, radio and television programme was scanned, and a reporter picked out. Each was contacted, met, and individually briefed, so that the press coverage of the launch was guaranteed before we began.

This intensive planning and person-to-person contact with the communications world paid off. Good public relations, for all its gin-and-tonic image is only achieved by hard work.

Enthusiasm breeds enthusiasm, and the idealism and the pace that was engendered into the campaign over the final weeks before the launch date created such a sense of urgency that it not only carried the SHELTER team through a nerve-racking time unscathed, but also got under the skin of many journalists who came into contact with the team, being reflected in the crusading zeal that many eventually carried into their reports.

All of this, and Cathy. The screening of Cathy just a few days before the launching of SHELTER was coincidental. We didn't know it was coming. Indeed, I was working late at the office that night, and didn't see the film until long after SHELTER was launched.

That SHELTER's launch would have been a success without Cathy I don't doubt, for the stage had been set by months of hard work. But Cathy created the atmosphere throughout the country that guaranteed the voice of SHELTER was not only heard at the beginning of December, but understood.

The Initial Response

January 10, 1967

"SHELTER has raised £50,000 in its first month. The response from all over Britain to its appeal for the homeless has been tremendously encouraging, it says, and in addition to the money flowing in there are hundreds of offers of help."

SHELTER was launched on a Thursday, and the SHELTER team was in Birmingham the following Monday night when the message came through—"We already have £7,000." By the following night when we were in Liverpool the total was over £10,000. Our pleasure at the news was mixed with relief—perhaps it was only at the moment of success that we realised what a risk it had all been.

The SHELTER Campaign had been launched without a penny in the bank, and if it had failed a number of people would have had to pay out of their own pockets, not least David Reid, our young Treasurer.

One full page of advertising in "The Times" set alongside a page of editorial matter, brought in a huge response—over £12,000. This figure has never been exceeded from a single ad. The Guardian ran a leader backing the campaign—*"This is almsgiving made businesslike, and deserves all support."* —and this no doubt contributed to the tremendous response. One ad, costing £300, brought in over £7,000. The response to all our advertising was fantastic.

By now we had been working nearly fifteen hours a day, seven days a week, for months. But somehow we found the energy to prepare a newsheet on the campaign's first week, and to post it to over 25,000 churches. It brought in nearly £10,000.

An Ideal Home

February 28, 1967

"One surprise in store for the million expected visitors to this year's Ideal Home Exhibition at Olympia is the exhibit from SHELTER. *The stand does* **not** *feature an ideal home–in fact, just the opposite. The centre-piece is a recreation of the one-room home of a family of six in Notting Hill.* SHELTER *wishes to remind sightseers around the best homes that Britain can create in 1967 that there are still three million families living in unsatisfactory housing conditions."*

Organising a stand at the Ideal Home Exhibition is a nightmare, particularly if you haven't got much money. Costs escalate, and voluntary manpower has to be organised. But for all that and despite the fact that it lost money, this did much to establish SHELTER as a campaign willing to jolt people out of their complacency. I've no doubt that it ruined the look of the 1967 Ideal Home Exhibition, but it heavily publicised the homeless, as well as being seen by hundreds of thousands of people.

The Return of Cathy

March 1, 1967

"The B.B.C. has granted the exclusive rights of the controversial "Cathy Come Home" for at least a year to SHELTER. *The play's author, Jeremy Sandford, has offered to forego his author's royalties for the year, and the cast are all co-operating, through Equity."*

Cathy had been shown again in January, and the uproar that followed was even greater than after the first showing.

Jeremy Sandford, the tall, curly-haired author of Cathy, was a great help. He tipped us off about the second showing well in advance, and we were able to mount an advertising campaign with a picture of Cathy and organise a press conference, attended by Jeremy. In addition, he and Carol White, who played Cathy, went to Olympia to sign copies of his book on the SHELTER stand.

I appeared with Jeremy on "The Frost Programme" that night. It was my first television appearance, and I suddenly realised that I had been so busy with SHELTER that I had never actually seen Cathy. Frost promised that I could watch it at the studio but when the time came I was so nervous that I hardly saw more than a minute. I only appeared on the programme briefly, but for one small family and myself it was a decisive appearance.

The following day about 2 p.m. the telephone rang in my office, and a man came on the line to say that he had just converted his house into two self-contained flats, and was prepared to reserve one of them for any family I nominated. Only minutes later there was a knock on the door, and a woman came in. That she was an expectant mother was only too apparent, and so I hastily sat her down and offered her a cup of tea. I was stunned when she burst into tears.

She explained to me that she and her husband were to be evicted because she was having a child. "We've got to be out by tomorrow, and I've been everywhere looking for a place. You're the first man to offer me anything–even a cup of tea," she said. Her story unfolded . . . of tramping the streets from one place to another all day, getting nothing but "no" for an answer and usually being sent from one welfare office to another without anybody bothering to telephone her destination to see whether the trip was worthwhile.

Up to that moment I had managed to remain reasonably detached, but now for the first time I got mad–really mad. I could hardly believe that our society had become so indifferent to the feelings of others that a mother, about to have a child any day, could be shunted around a huge and tiring city for a whole day without a smile from anyone.

Then I remembered the man who telephoned. I rang him back and he readily agreed to accept the couple. They went out there that night, and their problem was solved. It was the first family that I had myself helped to rehouse, and I don't know who was happier, she or I.

Walking for the Homeless

April 11, 1967

> "SHELTER *Walk Week reaches its climax this weekend when 90 groups of young people will take part in their own sponsored walks to raise money for Britain's homeless. Altogether some 160 walks were organised for Walk Week, and more than 6,000 young people took part. The most ambitious walk was the relay by 40 members of the Wokingham Methodist Youth Club from London to Glasgow–a distance of 400 miles."*

When we were planning SHELTER, I often raised the eyebrows of some of the less imaginative by talking about "nationalising" local fund raising activities. I pointed out that things like jumble sales had become traditional fundraisers for a simple reason–they nearly always worked. But why wait for people to organise jumble sales? Why not organise a multitude all on the same day and call it "The Jumble Sale of the Year". We could then justify promoting jumble sales as a big effort, and at the same time raise our money in "big lumps". We later did this, and managed to get over 400 jumble sales on one day in 1968.

But the first activity to be given what we called "the treatment" was the sponsored walk.

Sponsored walks had become the "in thing" in the mid-1960s. The idea was to get as many people walking as far as possible, with as many of their family and friends sponsoring them at 6d. or 1/- a mile as they could collect. The secret lay not in how many walkers you had, or how far they walked, but in the number of sponsors. Thus, a lad could walk 50 miles but if he only had four sponsors, at 6d. a mile, he would raise £5 where another one could walk 20 miles but because he had 50 sponsors at 6d. a mile he could raise £45.

Every school and youth club in the country was mailed, and "Walk Week" was, we thought then, a terrific success. I say "we thought then" because it grew in 1968 and 1969 until walks were raising at least £100,000 a year. Back in April, 1967, we were happy to think it might raise £20,000.

More than 40,000 people took part in the 1968 Walk Week, in over 450 walks. Over 380 boys from Malvern College, Worcester, collected 4,000 sponsors for their 30 mile walk and set up a record of £6,000 after Eileen Ware had been to speak at the school. Later Radley College, near Oxford, were to beat this after I had spoken to the senior boys. They raised nearly £7,000 with a walk!

A lot of concern has been expressed about the danger to road safety in sponsored walks, but SHELTER has practically made its walks exercises in road safety, providing extensive notes, and insisting that this be built into the organisation of every walk.

The lack of thought behind much of the anti-walk activity is underlined by the retiring Chief Constable for East Sussex who, at the time, accused young people of taking part in walks for "publicity stunts". One would have thought that an experienced policeman would know that if young people wanted publicity they could get it a lot more simply than walking fifty miles from London to Brighton. For instance, by chucking a brick through the Chief Constable's window!

Director of SHELTER

May 30, 1967

"The Trustees of SHELTER *National Campaign for the Homeless, today named 26 years-old Des Wilson as Director of* SHELTER *He has been* SHELTER's *Campaign Director since before its launch in December last year. He leads probably the youngest campaign team fielded by a major charity–average age about 24. By May 1967* SHELTER *had raised £125,000, established a fund of goodwill in the churches, among young people, and men and women who had been forming* SHELTER *groups.*

But internally, things weren't well. The Trustees still had not appointed a Director, and the organisation tended to drift without much sense of direction, to lose sight of its objectives, and to lack the kind of efficient, fully-equipped and forward-looking organisation needed to maintain its initial success. There was no permanent plan and we were living, in a sense, from day to day.

Up to then, I had carried the brunt of the day-to-day work, but the load had been fairly evenly shared, under the loose supervision of the Trustees, and mainly through their chairman, Bruce Kenrick.

Bruce Kenrick had been chairman of Notting Hill Housing Trust, and a driving force behind the launching of SHELTER. He had helped to raise the money for the launching, carried out most effectively the negotiations with the founding organisations, and acted as a spokesman for the campaign when it was launched.

There is little point in pretending that Bruce Kenrick and I hit it off well. We had worked closely and happily up until a few weeks before SHELTER was launched, but communication had broken down, and with it the basis for trust. The first half of 1967 had been fraught with tension, and things were to get worse rather than better.

Personality clashes in any kind of organisation, whether it be an industrial concern, a political movement, or a voluntary movement, are hardly unusual, but for some reason in voluntary movements they create a special kind of bitterness.

But we were sharing responsibility for a campaign that desperately cried out for one firm hand, and we had differing views about how the campaign could be developed at a time when it desperately needed a clear sense of direction.

In any event, by May '70, while Bruce Kenrick was still Chairman, the Trustees could wait no longer to appoint a permanent Director for the campaign, and, when David Reid put my name forward at a meeting that I did not attend, I was elected unopposed.

I set down and hammered out a Campaign Plan, and set to work to mould my own team.

I put the accent on a combination of idealism and professionalism. Nothing kills idealism more quickly, or disillusions and frustrates the idealist more, than the linking of ideals to inefficiency. To work on a full time team of charity, and expect to command a salary for it, it's not enough to care–you must have something specific and practical to offer.

And so the SHELTER team that exists now was born, with the arrival of Eileen Ware, Liz Wills, and Cindy Barlow.

By now we had become "grossly overcrowded" ourselves, and we moved to our present address at 86 The Strand, managing to get floor space at a reduced rate by moving in with the National Federation of Housing Societies in an ideal position, near to Fleet Street, Whitehall, and Westminster, radio and television headquarters, and two of the main London railway stations, Waterloo and Charing Cross. People often question whether we can justify the expense of being placed so centrally, but it would cost us more if we were not there. SHELTER has been built by and around the communications world, and it owes a lot to its close proximity to the media.

Shelter Groups

August 30, 1967

"SHELTER *now has 100 local Groups in villages, towns and cities spread through 36 countries in England, Scotland and Wales, its Groups Organiser, Liz Wills, said today."*

One of the first problems we were confronted with after the launching of SHELTER was what to do about the men and women all over Britain who had written in to say: "How can we help?"

If SHELTER was to succeed the headquarters team had to be backed up in local communities all over the country.

So it was decided to launch SHELTER Groups. Liz was given the task of building up the groups and co-ordinating their activities. We organised our first SHELTER Rally in June, 1967 and were excited by the enthusiasm that was shown.

"I must have travelled about 6,000 miles around Britain in that first year and some of the SHELTER team wondered if I had left for good!", Liz says.

Back to School . . .

September 14, 1967

Hundreds of thousands of children in Britain are going to school each day from housing conditions so oppressive that their capacity for education is severely restricted, claims an unusual report released today by SHELTER. *The campaign is vigorously drawing attention to the difficulties that face children living in slums. A 20-page report is made up almost entirely of*

> *comments from school-teachers and social workers working in the slum districts of Britain's worst hit housing cities, and copies have been sent to the Minister of Housing and the Minister of Education."*

The series of "shock reports" released by SHELTER in September of each year, between T.U.C. conference and the Liberal Party Conference, while the House of Commons is not sitting and when news is scarce, are a key part of the SHELTER formula.

Each year they form a re-launch of the campaign, and such is the publicity they attract that they not only launch the Autumn Appeal but their effects are still felt when the Christmas campaign is launched.

Further, by focusing attention on a fresh aspect of the housing problem, they guarantee that the public don't get bored with the permanent, on-going message of the campaign.

All that we learnt at the time of the launch of SHELTER and the additional lessons we learnt in September, 1967, go into making our Autumn campaign the main event of the SHELTER year.

Apart from anything else, I think the Autumn campaigns built round the reports are good for the SHELTER team itself, in two respects: firstly, they inject fresh life into the campaign boosting the morale of all concerned. Secondly, the research for the report injects fresh facts and ideas into every speech given for SHELTER and into every article written about it.

The idea for "Back to School from a Holiday in the Slums" came from Eileen Ware, and the secret of the report was its simplicity. Nearly every major newspaper splashed the report, and radio and television gave it massive coverage.

From this we launched our "House a Family for Christmas Campaign".

House a Family for Christmas

October 8, 1967

"SHELTER *has launched a "House a Family for Christmas Campaign". Churches of all denominations are being encouraged to raise in their district the sum of £325, sufficient when multiplied by loans and improvement grants to rehouse a family in urgent need. The campaign will culminate on Christmas Day."*

For the first three years of the campaign, the sum of £325 consistently remained the sum needed, on average, to rehouse an average-sized family in average circumstances, by the time the

housing association, with whom SHELTER worked, had borrowed money and obtained the various grants and subsidies.

The "House a Family for Christmas Campaign" really caught on, churches and schools picking up the idea.

The combination of the schoolchildren's report in September and the "House a Family for Christmas Campaign" were, in fact, the events that really put SHELTER on the map as a major charity, virtually doubling its income in a matter of weeks.

Perhaps the turning point was the brilliant advertising campaign devised by copywriter, Peter Hodgson, and designer, John Booth, at our advertising agency.

Instead of the usual, sentimental Christmas advertising, the agency chose to reflect the bitterness of families living in the slums at Christmastime. The headline said:

Christmas–You can stuff it for all I care

"Christmas–the bright lights, the big spend-up, the family get-togethers the sentimentality–it's an insult to a family like this.

You are looking at the hopeless, helpless anger of

> **Britain's three million slum dwellers. People who have been rejected so often that they reject everything.**
> **Yet, surely, the Christmas message was meant to bring hope to people like these.**
> **Get them out of their dreadful overcrowded rooms. Give them a decent home. Let them start living again. This is what SHELTER wants to do."**

All of this below a picture of a family standing in the doorway of a damp Glasgow tenement.

Some people were horrified. One of my Trustees said he could not defend it in public, and another said it was the equivalent of cutting up railway carriages after a football match.

But the ad was helped on its way by an article in *The Observer* written by Colin McGlashan, later to be named "Campaigning Journalist of the Year", who had been at the meeting when the agency presented me with the ad, and had been working on a story about SHELTER for some time.

McGlashan's article boosted SHELTER in two ways: firstly, it reflected the rawness of the campaign accurately and enthusiastically and in itself increased public goodwill. Secondly, it "sold" the idea of the Christmas advertising. His story began:

> **"The photograph in the dummy advertisement is raw: poverty without pathos. The headline is blunter still: Christmas? You can stuff it for all we care.**
> **"SHELTER the National Campaign for the Homeless, is one year old now and this week takes possibly its biggest gamble: debunking Christmas with a brutally direct advertising campaign that is a world and a half away from conventional tinselly images of the fundraisers best season.**
> **"That headline isn't going to arouse sympathy for the homeless,"says Des Wilson, SHELTER's Director and**

Britain's charity whizz kid. "It's going to hit people between the eyeballs. The copy's got to justify the headline."

"SHELTER is gambling that the public is ready to accept that for the old, the poor, the lonely, and the homeless, Christmas is the cruellest month–the time that rubs in the contrast between the haves and the have-nots. One ad is a photograph of a squalid lavatory cistern: "Christmas is a time for sharing. 23 people share this".

The risk is real. SHELTER's blunt unsentimental exposure of housing conditions has already flushed out those who see poverty as a crime. One ad drew a letter: "Some people might think sterilization is the first need."

"The campaign is crucial for SHELTER committed to raising £50,000 in the next five weeks. At its London offices, its young staff is keeping fingers crossed. It shares a youthful horror of self-perpetuating organisational structures ("We exist to work ourselves out of a job" says a notice). It works–sometimes from 8 a.m. till midnight in a state of amiable committed anarchy: staff (lots of pretty girls in mini-skirts) takes its own decisions, and local Groups are independent. Often the first Head Office knows of a fundraising drive is when the money rolls in.

"Wilson himself–a New Zealander and formerly a public relations man–sets SHELTER's tone: total involvement, bright ideas and no red tape.

"SHELTER is increasingly accepted as a current pioneer in the whoele charity field in the same way that Oxfam–which brought large scale advertising and efficiency to British fundraising–was in the late fifties. SHELTER represents a new young, aggresive face of charity, more attracted to protest marches than the rattle of a collecting box. Both SHELTER

and Oxfam are involving youngsters in such numbers that they now have a secondary role as major youth organisations."

I was later to defend this advertising in a paper to the Working Party on Charities set up by the National Council of Social Services:

"This ad was not attacking the festive season. Nor was it using strong language to shock just for the sake of shock. What it was doing was questioning the way we celebrate Christmas. We believe we could only express the bitterness of the poor by using the words of the people themselves. This was truthful. This was uncompromising. Certainly there was a risk that we might alienate some of our supporters. But we were truly representing the feelings of the people that we were formed as an organisation to represent . The response was that more money came in from that ad than for any other. And I believe it proved that people respond to truth. They respond to urgent need when it is presented to them in an urgent way.
We are asked whether the public is likely to react against more hard-hitting advertising. There may be a risk in this, but are they likely to respond to a rejection of present day methods and a return to the more conservative approach? Do we want charity to be neatly fitted into our society and not becoming so conspicious that people become uncomfortable, or do we want charities and voluntary organisations to express their concren and express the isolation of their beneficiaries in such a way that it cannot be ignored?"

Most observers will agree that this advertising campaign changed the face of British charity advertising, perhaps for ever.

Also at Christmas, 1967, B.B.C. television's "Blue Peter" children's programme decided to appeal for stamps for a SHELTER housing project and the response was phenomenal, more than 120 million stamps being collected. George Nicholson had to organise the count and he can tell you that's a lot. We were helped by prisoners in many of the country's jails, particularly the men in prison hospitals. Ken Bartlett, of the Paddington Churches Housing Association, carried out the house improvement exercise under television's spotlights, and even 7 year-old Prince Andrew had people at Buckingham Palace collecting stamps.

So it was that the first year of SHELTER came to an end.

First Year's Achievement

December 1, 1967

"SHELTER *is one year old today. Perhaps it has achieved more in its first year than any other charity in history–it has raised £200,000 got homes under way for well over 1,000 people, undertaken a persistent programme of publicity for the homeless, sending speakers to about 350 meetings, and screening the film, "Cathy Come Home" more than 400 times, launched over 100* SHELTER *Groups, and involved so many young people that it is practically a youth movement."*

In fact, the campaign year did not end until January 31, 1968 and by then, SHELTER had left its target £270,000 far behind, and in fact raised £370,041.

Human Rights

April 29, 1968

SHELTER *has rejected three donations–for £5, £20, and £35 respectively, because they were accompanied by the demand that they be used to help white*

> *people only, or by letters that were racialist in tone,* SHELTER's *constitution says: '. . . the Trust shall seek to play a creative part in the life of the nation by relieving human suffering irrespective of colour, creed or class . . . "*

1968 was Human Rights Year, and SHELTER agreed to be responsible for the provision of services to the Human Rights Year Housing Group. I was elected Chairman, and Eileen Ware, Secretary.

The year had begun quietly, with the youth campaign dominating most of our activities.

Powellism was rife in the country, and SHELTER began to get donations sent to it linked to racialist letters, and in some cases specifying that they go to help white families only.

SHELTER did not wish to be involved in racial controversy of any kind, recognising that even though its intentions might be good, it could actually be adding fuel to the fire.

On the other hand, it is our belief that all people resident in Britain are entitled to a decent home as a human right, and we couldn't in all conscience accept a donation that makes the pursuance of that policy impossible. Further, we felt that the majority of our supporters would want us to make our position clear, even though we might lose a little money as a result of it.

And so I brought the matter up at a meeting of my Trustees, and it only took two minutes to get their approval for me to send back three donations and to publicise the fact.

Vietnam Cared

May 30, 1968

> *A donation has been received by* SHELTER *from the Overseas Missionary Fellowship in Saigon. The*

cheque for £ll.lO.O. is accompanied by a letter saying: 'We have hesitated to send a donation at the time when the needs of the homeless here in Vietnam are so great but we feel that the need here is much more widely known.'"

SHELTER had now reached its first half a million pounds and the sum of £11.10.0. may seem small. But coming from a country being torn apart by war, and where the suffering was so great, this particular donation is one I shall never forget.

Ha'pennies for the Homeless

August 8, 1968

"Even a halfpenny can help the homeless–especially when it is multiplied 960 million times. That's the message Britain is sending out to Britain's children as a result of the news that 960 million halfpennies now in circulation will be collector's items only after August, 1969."

Jo McBride, who was our hard working research organiser for a couple of years, spotted in "The Sun" that halfpennies were to go out of circulation in a year, and within 48 hours we had printed a leaflet and begun to distribute it among children all over the country.

We had learned, as a result of the Blue Peter exercise, how much kids love collecting things, and our faith in them was not misplaced this time..

By July 30, 1969, the young people of Britain had collected a fantastic six and a half million halfpennies–enough to rehouse 45 needy families.

Rally in the Rain

August 12, 1968

"At a Rally in Trafalgar Square on Sunday,

September 15, thousands of Londoners are expected to show their support for Britain's homeless–half a million of whom live within Greater London. The theme of the Rally which falls on "Battle of Britain Day" will be "The New Battle for Britain–make housing a human right."

I will refer to the "Notice to Quit" Autumn campaign in Chapter 10, but can't resist putting in an extract from the press release, if only to show that the best plans can go astray.

September 15, 1968, saw the most torrential rainfall Britain had experienced for years, and the scene in Trafalgar Square can only be described as pathetic. The rain was coming down in bucketloads, and the handful of speakers at our first Rally, together with press representatives, outnumbered the crowd. Nevertheless, every speaker insisted on having his say, and most spoke for more than the time that had been allotted for them, even when we had hoped for sunshine. The result was that the Rally got all the publicity one could have hoped for on a good day and the speakers, after wringing out their wet clothes in a nearby coffee bar–were able to go home with a feeling of achievement as well as martyrdom.

Following the Autumn campaign, SHELTER had its first "Week". This was a bit of a cheek, but again it achieved its dual objectives–firstly, to raise money, and secondly, to underline the growing importance of SHELTER. As someone commented to me at the time: "Any charity that names a week after itself has either made it or deserves it for sheer nerve!"

SHELTER in Scotland

October 3, 1968

"SHELTER *today launched a permanent Scottish campaign for the homeless. Its sponsors include the*

Lord Provosts of Aberdeen, Dundee, Edinburgh, and Glasgow, leading politicians and church figures, and show business personalities. A special Scottish Advisory Council to handle policy aspects of its campaign, chaired by David Steel, M.P., Scottish Organiser for SHELTER *32 years old Ronald Dick, who handles the campaign from headquarters in Castle Street, Edinburgh."*

The housing problem in Scotland is unique in its ugliness and in the way that it dominates the social life of the country.

So is Scotland unique, having its own housing legislation. a housing terminology of its own and–let's face it–strong nationalistic inclinations.

For some time it had been clear to SHELTER that if we were going to make the impact we should make in Scotland, we would need to "wear a kilt". And so it was decided to open an office in Edinburgh, and launch SHELTER separately in Scotland. This we did with a bang, getting massive television and press coverage, and immediately boosting the morale of the movement, such as it was, in Scotland

It was decided that all the money raised in Scotland would be spent in Scotland, and we were fortunate in getting together a particularly strong Avisory Council.

Ronald Dick, a pugnacious and versatile man with a stubborn streak that made him ideal for the post, quickly built round him a tough and loyal team that raised nearly £100,000 in its first years.

1969 Youth Campaign

January 1, 1969

"Young people from 110,000 schools, colleges, youth clubs in England, Scotland, and Wales have been asked to take part in a massive campaign to raise

> *money for the homeless through* SHELTER; *The target for each group is at least £325.".*

The 1969 Youth campaign, launched on New Year's Day involved a Walk Week, a halfpenny collection, a Tiny Tots Painting Competition, and a "Tycoon Competition".

The basis of the last-mentioned acitivity is that each boy or girl would be given 2/6d. by their mum or dad, and given a fortnight to make the money grow. This project came from a group of young people in Surrey who had become SHELTER "Tycoons" for a fortnight in 1968, raising £600–almost enough to rehouse two families. Only one boy came back with nothing–he put his half a crown on a horse and it lost!

Eileen Ware achieved £250,000 with her youth campaign in the year–enough to rehouse 950 families!

The First Million

January 7, 1969

> "SHELTER *has raised its first one million pounds. This has been achieved in 25 months, nearly nine months ahead of the original target date."*

SHELTER was to go on to raise over £700,000 in its second campaign year, bringing its income to £1,075,000. Overheads had been reduced from 19 per cent to 16 per cent.

The Eton Campaign

March 13, 1969

> *"Boys at Eton College are to campaign for Britain's homeless. The activities over four days are to be run by a new group called Eton Action, a committee set up by boys and masters. Events will include a collection from the boys at the College, a sponsored walk, a private pop concert, and a street market."*

Francis Carnwath, Treasurer of SHELTER and a former

pupil of Eton, arranged for Eileen Ware to speak at the College about the work of SHELTER and SHELTER became the first charity to be supported by a major campaign at the College. It not only raised over £5000 but also attracted massive publicity.

£25,000 Gift

April l4,1969

"SHELTER *has been given an anonymous gift of £25,000. The second highest sum donated to* SHELTER *so far.*"

Apart from a massive gift of £50,000 for a specific project in Bradford, there was the second highest gift donated to SHELTER. The next highest was £10.000 and apart from the money raised by activities such as walks, the average size of donations to SHELTER is in fact around the £5 mark.

I am often asked why SHELTER doesn't concentrate on raising more money in lump sums. Apart from the fact that this is not easy, we have deliberately aimed our campaign at raising the maximum amount of money from the maximum number of people, believing involvement through giving is as important as the money raised. To put it bluntly, given the choice between a million pounds from one millionare or a million pounds from a million people, I would choose the latter, because of the commitment to the homeless that it would involve.

Not, I hasten to add, that I would turn the million away!

The Big Debate

April 1968

"Des Wilson, Director of SHELTER, *debates with Richard Crossman, Secretary of State for Health and Social Security, at Cambridge University tonight. He will propose the motion: "That poverty in Britain is self-perpetuating and meant to be so."*

I had looked forward to the debate with Crossman for some time and what a battle it turned out to be. He won. But not easily. By 144 votes to 113.

A reporter from "The Guardian" began his account as follows:

> **"The motion was ungrammatical, one or two purists grumbled, in the Cambridge Union gallery last night. No matter, so were the battle cries of Roman gladiators. And the Union, for a rare moment in its history, was an arena.**
>
> **For the first time it let loose Mr. Des Wilson, the vehement and successful young director of "Shelter" the National Campaign for the Homeless, on the man who at one time or another has masterminded policy in all the Government departments with which Mr. Des Wilson is angry–Mr. Richard Crossman, M.P. sometime Minister of Housing, now Secretary for Health and Social Security.**
>
> **The motion, "that poverty in Britain is self-perpetuating and meant to be so "was a savage rejection of gradualist reform. In proposing it, Mr. Wilson, a New Zealander who had never been to university or debated, pitted himself against an ex-Oxford don, who is one of the virtuoso debaters of his generation. Mr. Wilson was slightly scared–but he went hewing at the motion with a sword of outrage, while Mr. Crossman waited in ambush with the trident of logic and the net of Ministerial statistics."**

Commented "Varsity":

> **"The real victor of the evening was the noble art of debating. The analogy of a dignified, almost courtly conflict. cannot be overdone."**

Professor Peter Townsend and I were to take on Crossman again in 1970–this time our motion of "little confidence" in the Administrations poverty measures won the night by some 25 votes.

Lord Harlech's Arrival

May 5, 1969

"The success or failure of our modern society will be determined by how we deal with the problems of our cities." The Rt. Hon. Lord Harlech, former Ambassador to the United States, told businessmen at a SHELTER *Lunch held at the Guildhall today."*

SHELTER had made little impression on the business world, and lunches organised in London, Birmingham, and Liverpool were aimed at rectifying this.

I had met Lord Harlech at a speak out on race organised by the National Council for Civil Liberties and asked him to help. He readily agreed, and spoke effectively at all the lunches. Later he became Honarary Chairman of SHELTER and one of the Turstees.

About this time, Eamonn Casey, who had been a magnificent chairman, both in terms of his working relationship with myself and the SHELTER team, and in terms of his popularity among SHELTER supporters, was made Bishop of Kerry, and Lewis Waddilove, another one of the founder Trustees, took over the post of Executive Chairman of the Trustees.

Much of the credit for the way the Trustees delegated responsibility to the SHELTER team, and stood by it through thick and thin, goes to Eamonn Casey, who in the eighteen months or so of the chairmanship had played a major part in every aspect of SHELTER's work, whilst always making it clear that he was there when called upon, rather than there to interfere.

Earlier in the year, journalist Adam Fergusson had helped Eamonn to write "A Home of Your Own", a paperback published by SHELTER offering advice to young people about housing, and this, together with the launching of the SHELTER Housing Aid Centre in 1970, as a culmination of his work with the Catholic Housing Aid Society, brought Eamonn Casey's work for the homeless to a most satisfactory climax.

The Sprinting Snail

July 25, 1969

"A record-breaking sprinting snail, sponsored by SHELTER *will challenge the world on Tuesday, the 5th in an International Snail Race. It will take place on a glass track, specially constructed for the event, on the sands at Folkestone. A record time for the 24 inch track stands at a stunning 19 minutes and 35 seconds."*

One of the incongruities of running a campaign like SHELTER is that you can find yourself issuing a serious press release commenting on the activities of the Ministry of Housing one day, and the results of a snail race the next (not that their speed always differs!).

Snail racing came upon us in July, 1969, and its success owes much to a series of hilarious press releases written by Richard Plumridge, in our Press Office.

In the autumn came SHELTER's "Face the Facts" campaign, discussed in full in chapter 10.

September 19, 1969

"The Archbishop of Canterbury, Dr, Michael Ramsey has asked for a collection for SHELTER *to be made at the Service to commemorate his 40 years as ordained priest."*

The Archbishop of Canterbury has been most generous to SHELTER and he marked his enthusiasm for the campaign by choosing it for the collection on this personal occasion. Previously, he had chaired a British Council of Churches meeting at Plymouth when I had the opportunity of addressing church leaders from all over the country.

Two resolutions passed on that occasion underlined the backing given to the campaign by the churches.
They were:

> **"The Council welcomes the link between the British Churches Housing Trust and SHELTER and commends SHELTER to all its member Churches for their continued support"**
>
> **"The Council records its grateful appreciation of the services rendered by SHELTER in raising over £1,000,000 since the inception of its campaign in December 1966, in bringing the plight of the homeless to the notice of the public, and in making representations on this matter to H.M. Government."**

Also in September SHELTER had a successful B.B.C. television appeal. This was made by Kenneth Allsop and, in Scotland, actor John Fraser spoke for SHELTER. Together they raised over £25,000.

Three Years Old

December 1, 1969

> "SHELTER *is three years old today and is now helping to rehouse three families every single day. In its three years* SHELTER *has raised over £1,750,000 and confidently expects to reach a second million by the end of its campaign year, January 31, 1970. The campaign is at least £500,000 ahead of its target, and helped 2,337 families to a better home and has homes in the pipeline for at least another 2,405 families. It now aims to reach its target of £1 million a year in 1970."*

In fact, SHELTER raised over one million pounds in 1969 alone and reached that 12 months target a year ahead of schedule. By then it had raised in all £2,100,000.

Its housing operation would always need to be seen in the context of the larger problems that remained. Its pressure activities could be assessed, but their effectiveness would always be a matter of opinion.

But at least one objective could be clearly defined: the fund raising target. And that objective has been achieved!

NINE

December 1, 1966

"The bulk of the money raised by the SHELTER Campaign will be distributed among highly-efficient housing associations co-operating with the local authorities in Britain's four worst-hit cities–London, Glasgow, Birmingham and Liverpool. These voluntary, non-profitmaking local groups buy houses, convert them into good simple homes, and let them at fair rents to families in urgent need."

SHELTER Press Release

THE SHELTER STORY (2): RESCUE

There are a variety of different types of housing associations, societies, and trusts, and I don't wish to bore you with all the variations. SHELTER's rescue operation is restricted to non-profitmaking voluntary housing associations, themselves registered as charities, and concerned, to quote the aims and objects of the Notting Hill Housing Trust, "to provide good simple homes for families and old people who are either homeless or living in conditions of overcrowding, and to help rehabilitate that minority of tenants who need assistance with family and social problems".

As the extract from our first press release (above) shows, SHELTER policy for the first year or so was based on three principles:

Firstly, we chose to work through existing housing associations, instead of beginning our own. Whilst there were administrative advantages to setting up our own housing groups, this would have wasted expertise and experience already existing.

But the main reason why we resisted the idea of a nation-wide housing organisation, with all the power concentrated at 86 The Strand, was that we wanted our money spent according to the specific circumstances of each city and we wanted a situation where the control was spread as widely as possible.

SHELTER has never sought power, and this is to be seen both in its relationship with the housing associations, and in the way it set up the Neighbourhood Action Project in Liverpool and the Housing Aid Centre in London, both run independently of SHELTER with their own boards of Trustees.

The second principle was to concentrate on a small number of housing associations, to enable them to become more professional, and thus able to form the backbone, of the SHELTER housing programme over a number of years. Of the seven chosen, one has fallen by the wayside, but the other six now figure among the biggest housing associations in the country, mainly as a result of this injection of SHELTER money in 1967/68.

The third principle was to concentrate the bulk of SHELTER money on only four cities–London, Birmingham, Liverpool, and Glasgow. Although an ambulance service was required all over the country, in these cities the situation was totally out of control, and this was where extra help was most urgently needed.

We knew this last policy decision would weigh against us when raising money, for people like to raise money for their own town and city, and often resent it going to another. But Britain's housing problem is a problem of blackspots, and if SHELTER was to ignore this in its own operation, it would lose all credibility in its campaign to get the authorities to look at it in the proper light.

Nearly all of the SHELTER money goes to housing associations to carry out a programme of rehabilitation and conversion. The associations don't only rescue people, but also properties, and every house brought up to standard, and properly maintained, indirectly increases the housing stock.

They employ a number of full-time professionals, with skills in house purchase, rehabilitation and conversion, house management, and welfare. If the association is working with SHELTER in a big way and has not been able to afford to employ such people, SHELTER makesthe money available and insists that it does, for highly-developed skills are essential if the association is going to achieve the maximum return for the minimum money invested. It's no task for amateurs.

The Notting Hill Housing Trust

> *"Since the inception of the Notting Hill Housing Trust in December 1963, housing associations like the Trust have moved from the position where they were grateful for the opportunity to rehouse perhaps a dozen families in a year to a point where they can now plan realistically in terms of providing for the housing needs of hundreds of families in a year."*

Notting Hill Housing Trust's sixth report–September 1969.

The Notting Hill Housing Trust was the fatest–growing housing association when SHELTER was launched and was itself raising a lot of gift money.

I've chosen to take a special look at this housing

association, for although no association is typical, it does indicate how the SHELTER housing programme works at local level.

To understand the work of the Notting Hill Housing Trust, it is important to understand the background to its operation–Notting Hill itself.

Writing of Notting Hill in the Milner Holland Report, Ruth Glass said:

> **"Here are the people who must stay near their work in the centre, who cannot afford to move to the suburbs. Here are families who are at the tail-end of the municipal housing queues: and also those who are not eligible for such housing . . . here are immigrants from other parts of Britain or overseas . . . here is a motley collection of people who are pushed into the twilight zones. All of them have one thing in common: their housing needs are being exploited, and the very frictions which their crowded, insecure situation created, tend to be exploited too."**

Notting Hill lies to the north of the Royal Borough of Kensington and Chelsea, and its housing consists mainly of three, four, and five-storey Victorian terraced houses, usually with basements. Originally middle-class dwellings, the rooms are large and ideal for room-by-room letting. For the same reason the houses are reasonable sound structurally, and most do not qualify for slum clearance.

What has happened can be summed up by the Milner Holland Report that said:

> **"There is evidence of a new type of landlord entering the field, one interested primarily in speculation rather than investment, with relatively small holdings, operating mainly in multi-occupied property . . . unless steps are taken to make it easier for families either to buy or rent accommodation appropriate to their needs there must inevitably be an**

increase in the number of families overcrowded in unsuitable multi-occupied property . . .

In our own report, "Notice to Quit":

"All of the outward signs of multiple-occupation and neglect are there to be seen by any passer-by . . . mouldering brickwork, chunks of stone missing from the steps, streets littered, pavements uneven, dirty puddles, vacant lots filled with rubbish, phone boxes defaced and out of order, neglected gardens, gates and iron railings missing, steps decayed, rusty battered and overflowing dustbins, lidless dustbins covered with flies, scattered milk bottles, broken glass on roads and pavements, broken windows, lavatory doors missing, derelict cats and old furniture dumped in the streets.

"Some even manage to see something romantic in all this, but those who go inside these buildings soon come face to face with reality.

"Here families are waking, dressing, washing, eating, living and sleeping in single rooms. To quote the Milner Holland Report (still far too relevant): 'Large numbers of people are living in conditions which are more akin to those prevailing in the middle of the 19th century.'

" Many of the families are in desperate need. They say they have been told there is little chance of a local authority home for ten years. And they have to be in the borough for five years before they even get on a waiting list. Their low income has to meet high rents and is just sufficient to feed the family, although often inadequately. Property taking children is so hard to find that they cling to the appalling conditions and tolerate the occasional ill-treatment because the alternative could be even worse. The nerves of the parents reach breaking point. The

children are nagged by ill-health. Although their rents may be out of all proportion to the miserable accommodation they are cheaper than will have to be paid in better and less overcrowded areas in London. So these people cannot easily move elsewhere. The competition for any sort of housing leads to exploitation. Most of the housing is let furnished, so there is little security of tenure. The families live not just with insecurity but with fear."

When I was doing my original research for SHELTER I jotted down in the notebook and details of some families that I met and talked to in Notting Hill. Some of my notes follow:

"Mr. and Mrs. O'C., St. Stephens Gardens. This Irish couple with six children aged from 2 to 16 were paying £6.10.0 for two rooms in Colville Square, sharing a lavatory with 18 people. They moved to their present 'home' with two rooms and a kitchen for £7.10.0. Five of the children of both sexes, three of whom are teenagers, sleep in one room, three sisters, in one double bed. The Chief Medical Social Worker at their hospital has written, 'I feel that Mrs. O'C struggles so manfully against such overwhelming odds that for her sake and for that of her children, something should be done as soon as possible about their appalling situation.' "

"Mr. and Mrs. D., Bassein Park Road. Two parents and five children, one on probation at the age of 14, all live in one room just large enough to take the contents–one bed for three children, a put-u-up for the parents, a camp bed and a baby's cot. There is no floor space and the children have to play on the beds when indoors. Water has to be fetched from elsewhere in the house. Problem: appalling over-

crowding, children getting into trouble, and health and morale of family deteriorating. Probation Officer supervising the eldest child attributes his behaviour partly to lack of living space and privacy."

"Mrs. B., Elgin Crescent. She and her 8 year old daughter live in one room and a tiny kitchenette. A prostitute lives next door and the mother is terrified of the effect on the little girl's mind that the proximity might have. They share the w.c. with the prostitute and her clients, and pay £4 rent out of an income of about £10."

"Mr. and Mrs.W., Blenheim Crescent. Five living in one room. Rent £4.15.0. Whole flat unhealthy–smell of drains is dreadful, mice, dampness has caused paper to peel off the walls, floor dangerous and children often ill and have bug bites. Mrs. W.'s nerves are near breaking point (earlier in the year she attempted suicide)."

This, then, was the background to the formation of the Notting Hill Housing Trust in December, 1963.

The Royal Borough of Kensington and Chelsea, has, like all inner London Boroughs, many special problems. But even if one takes them into account, the Borough's record in tackling its housing problem shows a lack of resolution.

If they showed the same enthusiasm for meeting the needs of the homeless as they do in defending their record, it is conceivable they would have something worth defending.

At the time when the Notting Hill Housing Trust was launched, the local authority was devoting most of its efforts to slum clearance, and there was little hope of help to the majority of families living in slums outside development schemes. Furthermore. the local authority refused to re-house furnished tenants from redevelopment areas, and they were forced to seek refuge in the already overcrowded parts of Notting Hill.

A group of individuals, many of them with first hand knowledge of the housing conditions of Notting Hill and the social consequences of poor housing, decided that the situation could be tolerated no longer: and they determined to raise money to buy and improve houses and let them at rents that tenants could afford without being reduced to extreme poverty.

The gift money it raised for itself, and now gets from SHELTER as well, is used for: 1. Making good the difference between the cost of buying and converting a house, and the loans and subsidies received via the local authorities. 2. Rebating the rents of the poorest tenants. 3. The professional management of the association. 4. Welfare work.

The Committee, all voluntary, is chaired by a High Court Judge, and includes a management consultant, a solicitor, a barrister, a chartered surveyor, an architect, a chartered accountant, a social worker, and two housewives. The Citizens Advice Bureau and the Family Service Unit are both represented on the committee.

In this structure you can see both the strength and weakness of a housing association. The strength is that it brings professional expertise into a neglected area. The weakness is that its committee is unrepresentative of the kind of families rehoused. This is meant not so much in criticism of the past, as a pointer to where the association could expand its role in the years ahead.

Its manager, John Coward, is probably the most able and experienced manager of a housing association in the country. Working in Notting Hill, among a great variety of voluntary organisations and political movements, is like walking a tightrope over a mine field: John Coward is almost unique in commanding the respect of everybody in the district. both because of his professional ability, and his patience and open minded approach to radical suggestions. He plays a major part in the whole voluntary housing movement, being a Trustee of SHELTER, Chairman of a Committee that distributes SHELTER money to housing associations, as well as being Chairman of several other committees responsible for negotiating with national and local authorities.

To some entent the Notting Hill Housing Trust has held back a little of its own achievement in order to make available its expertise to the rest of the movement, and to undertake specific experiments, such as the running of its own rent rebate scheme.

For a number of years N.H.H.T. occupied an old house in Blenheim Crescent, but this became hopelessly overcrowded with full-time workers and volunteers, and so when some land became available, they built a block of 21 flats in All Saints Road, and incorporated their offices on the ground floor.

By February, 1970, the N.H.H.T. had permanently rehoused 1,567 people, and a further 167 people were occupying houses it owned (but had not yet converted) on an emergency basis, or who had been in possession when the house was purchased.

From five houses in 1964, the N.H.H.T. had moved to a point where it owned 202 houses in all, and was planning a major expansion that might triple the number within a year.

Of all the tenants, 122 were single people, 62 people were in couples, 68 were 1-child families, 100 were 2-child families, 53 were 3-child families, 30 were 4-child families, and 46 were larger families. Altogether 452 families had been rehoused, and 107 were in houses awaiting conversion, a total of 559.

As I said earlier the subsidy system has been loaded against the larger family, and this consistently worried the

N.H.H.T. for it had only been able to help a small number of large families, and in April, 1967 had even been forced to close down its waiting list for them.

As it said in its Report:

> **"Over the whole of the intervening period, a melancholy stream of families has called at our offices to make enquiries and, whilst it has been a great satisfaction to provide adequate housing for an increasing number of families, it has been a depressing task to have daily to turn away unhappy and sometimes desperate people over so long a period."**

Tenants are selected by a small and expert committee, having been visited by a welfare worker. The N.H.H.T. operates its own waiting list, trying always to give priority to those in greatest need. Because rigid points systems and red tape are unnecessary, they are more sensitive to need than any other kind of housing authority or organisation.

SHELTER has been pushing welfare as an essential part of housing associations, and the N.H.H.T. has been in the forefront, for it has always recognised that re-housing does not alleviate the anxieties and tensions that can develop during prolonged existence in overcrowded conditions, and many families require assistance with a whole range of problems. Loneliness and isolation, poverty and inability to provide furniture, curtains, or floor coverings when moving from small furnished to larger unfurnished housing, and inability to cope with gas cookers and other appliances, are all problems that are met and tackled.

A group of voluntary visitors help the family social worker to befriend a number of families, visiting and giving them help and encouragement. A panel of visitors also befriend lonely elderly people.

Many families face difficulties at the moment of re-housing often being unable to furnish their flat without help. For example, a family may have been paying as much as £7 rent for a furnished room out of a weekly wage of

£16 or £17. They have, in spite of this, generally managed to gather together their own crockery, cutlery, and bedding but have not furniture and, without help, would be faced with taking on hire purchase. The N.H.H.T. accepts good second-hand furniture and passes it on. Community Service Volunteers help here, and also collect and deliver furniture, help with jobs like laying lino, or putting up curtain rails for elderly people or women living on their own.

The volume of voluntary work reached a point where a full-time organiser was needed, and over one period of five weeks 156 volunteers worked on one or more occasions in fifteen properties, totalling approximately 950 hours work.

The N.H.H.T. is one of the larger, in terms of management, for John Coward has an assistant housing manager, a building foreman with a staff of 15 (reducing the costs of improvement and conversions substantially), a welfare officer and rent collector, an applications and lettings assistant, and administrative staff. They are always hopelessly overcrowded.

Help from the Authorities

March 9, 1967

"New measures in the Housing Subsidies Bill announced by the Minister of Housing last night mean that SHELTER *can house almost twice as many families with the money it raises."*

The main effect of SHELTER money is to trigger off the various loans, grants and subsidies that can be obtained from local authorities, for the role of housing associations has been recognised practically by the creation of many incentives.

The Housing Subsidies Bill 1967 meant thatinstead of borrowing money at what was the equivalent of over 7% SHELTER-type housing associations were able to borrow it, in effect, at just over 4%. This was the result of strong pressure brought by SHELTER and others, for the Bill in its unamended form gave help to housing associations building new homes, but no additional help to associations carrying out rehabilitation. An amendment was finally agreed, and this was to make a substantial difference to what could be achieved with SHELTER money.

In the three years that SHELTER has existed both national and local authorities have been bombarded with evidence of the difficulties that housing associations have to overcome, and pressure has led to much streamlining of the system, and more generous assistance.

In 1970 the G.L.C. was gradually introducing a scheme to enable massive expansion of housing associations.

The effect of the loans and subsidies has been that only about £325 of SHELTER money has been required to rehouse a family. This average figure was worked out in 1966 and, despite increasing costs, this has remained consistent over the first three years and is now being reduced.

Achievement

March 1, 1970

"SHELTER *has helped to re-house 3,103 families in co-operation with voluntary housing associations, and homes for another 2,840 are in the pipeline. Thus, when the present housing programme is complete, just under 6,000 families will have been re-housed, but this figure is expected to be increased still further by the end of 1970.*"

SHELTER money has helped to re-house an average of three families a day since is was launched, but as it took over nine months for the influx of money to SHELTER to begin to have real effect on housing associations, this housing programme has really been carried out over about two and a half years, and shows something of the impact of SHELTER in terms of rescuing families.

No one should overlook the relief of distress and misery that lies behind the figures. How many who scoff at money-raising can offer a practical solution to the problems of one family, let alone 6,000.

For 6,000 families, hope where there was no hope before. For 6,000 families, a home where there was a spiritless hell. For 6,000 an equal chance where before there was social oppression.

When all 6,000 homes are completed and when the families move in SHELTER's achievement will be spelled out in the strain lifted from faces most of its supporters will never see, colour brought into the lives of children they will never meet, and opportunity brought to families in communities they will never know.

That is the human impact of SHELTER and it is also found in the revitalised voluntary housing movement–in the new breed of effective, spirited, and powerful associations emerging from the trauma of our twilight zones, able to buy and convert faster, able to negotiate for better deals from the councils with SHELTER's punch behind them, able to get better borrowing facilities because of the security SHELTER offers, and able to plan ahead because they know the money is coming in.

The Case For and Against Housing Associations

SHELTER's achievement, and the work of housing associations, was marked by the Prime Minister, the Rt. Hon. Harold Wilson, who in March, 1970, opened some SHELTER financed houses in Birmingham.

Families with altogether 17 children were moving from overcrowded and damp flats and rooms into their newly-converted flats, and he spent over an hour at the dwellings handing the keys to the door of their new home to one of the tenants, Mr. Davies, and his wife and three children.

The Prime Minister's presence was particularly reassuring, in view of the growing controversy over the role of housing associations. He said:

> **"Let us dispute the prizes for those who can lead in the housing statistics. But inasmuch as you have provided these homes and many besides–and will provide still more–for those who might have felt themselves ignored by the most dedicated efforts of official bodies, your work deserves acclaim, and justifies a proud sense of achievement."**

This came at a time when the left-wing of the Labour Party had been firing warning shots across the bows of housing associations. It's not that they had condemned them, more that they were showing an increasing suspicion.

This suspicion was based on the coincidence between the expansion of housing associations and the fall-off in council house building, and further aroused by the enthusiastic support that the Conservatives were giving to housing associations. The Left's attitude seemed to be: "If the Tories are for them, there must be something wrong with them."

But whatever their motives, they were entitled to ask the questions, and indeed SHELTER had been asking them already. The Trustees at a meeting late in 1969 agreed that whilst there was no evidence that the cutback in housing by local authorities was in any way related to the expansion of the work of housing associations because of the assistance given by SHELTER, SHELTER had to devise a policy for dealing with any attempt that might be made to exploit its existence and the work of the housing associations with whom it was working. It was agreed that in allocating substantial sums of money to a housing association, SHELTER should be assured that this would not adversely affect the provision of housing, where that provision was needed by the private and public sector.

It was decided that if evidence was received that a local authority was reducing the scale of its own programme, because of the work of SHELTER, SHELTER would discontinue to contribute to the work of housing associations in that local authority's area.

Because SHELTER money was aimed at creating additional housing, and not letting local authorities off their own responsibilities, it was agreed that under no circumstances would we make available money to assist housing associations to take over either the ownership or management of existing council-built property. If a housing association wanted to do this, it would have to keep seperate accounts of its administrative expenditure, so that no SHELTER money whatsoever went into the project.

(Where a housing association is undertaking some activities that SHELTER would not itself be happy with, it is not always for SHELTER to stop it doing so, but rather for SHELTER to make it clear that the money given to that housing association by SHELTER cannot be spent on those activities.)

One of the things that has always concerned me has been that local authorities have the right to nominate a percentage of the tenants of housing associations. The authorities take the view that as they are providing anything up to 90% of the money, they should have this right. I have always felt that one of the unique contributions of the housing association is its ability to act as ab ambulance service and anything that reduces its capacity makes it less of an alternative to the authorities, and more part of them.

So while SHELTER accepts that it is sometimes right for housing associations to let their homes in agreement with the local authority, it was decided to oppose wholly the local authorities who insisted on nominating tenents for all the homes. Furthermore, housing associations, as charitable bodies, have been told to insist that they only re-house families that meet their aims and objects, so that if the local authority wants to nominate families, they must be families as equally in need as any other family on the association's waiting list.

In linking housing association growth with cutbacks in council house building, the left-wing overlooked the fact that there had also been a fall-off in every other aspect of housing. The building of houses for owner/occupiers and the provision of housing for private landlords have also fallen back, the latter fading away at the rate of about one-sixth and now controlling only 19 per cent of the housing stock. At the same time rising costs and the difficulty in obtaining home loans has taken house purchase out of the range of an increasing number of families.

I would say that the expansion of the housing association movement at a time when all other sectors were falling back was more due to single-minded determination than any other factor.

If we examine, for instance, the G.L.C. decision to make available £25 million a year for housing associations in London, there is adequate evidence that this was brought in as additional money, and in no way intended to cut back the G.L.C's own programme of house provision, inadequate though it might be.

In fact, because the money will be spent mainly on the purchase of houses on the open market in a variety of boroughs in London, in effect the G.L.C. is promoting housing associations in the place of the private landlord. If councils are to concentrate on slum clearance as well as building on every available piece of land, somebody has to be responsible for the maintenance and rehabilitation of our existing property. As it is no longer economic for the private landlords to do this if modest rents are charged, housing associations are the obvious answer, and because of their non-profitmaking structure they are often able to rehouse families from sub-standard conditions at a rent that is similar to what they were paying before.

Many people argue that the councils should extend their role not only owning new housing, but also buying up existing property, and becoming the landlord of that. But this creates the one-landlord borough, or city. If you ask David Mumford, the Manager of Birmingham Housing Trust (who is so left-wing in his politics that he has even been expelled once from the Labour Party) why he devotes his time to a housing association, you will find that instead of taking the traditional left-wing view that the council is the ideal landlord, he believes that the housing association is needed primarily as an alternative landlord.

Birmingham City Council is possibly the biggest landlord in the country, and dominates the housing field in Birmingham. Mumford points out that this makes the more vulnerable families as susceptible to the political variations of its landlord as it was previously susceptible to the behaviour of its private landlord. Housing associations create choice.

One should say that none of the leading politicians in any of the parties go along with the criticism of housing associations as letting the local authorities off the hook. Indeed, the Minister of Housing, Anthony Greenwood, when sent a copy of our policy document, wrote back to me:

> **"I was particularly pleased to see that SHELTER does not intend automatically to cutback aid to housing associations operating in areas where the local authority may be dragging its feet. Where a local authority has been lagging behind with its housing problem, the answer is continued pressure on it from all concerned."**

Socialists also are concerned about the spread of housing associations from the point of view of rent. There may be some truth in the fact that housing associations push up the rents, but how valid is the criticism? A housing association, being non-profitmaking is only charging the rent necessary to make itself economically viable, and it is not unfair to expect families, where they can afford to do so, to pay this rent. The answer to the poorer families is to extend the rent rebate scheme or housing subsidies across the whole housing board, so that the poorer families can be helped to pay the rents. Nobody will benefit from a housing association going bankrupt.

But a housing association, anyway, is not totally in control of its rent structure, as this has to be approved by the local authority, and therefore is under public control.

Whilst on this question of left-wing criticism that housing associations let the authorities off the hook, one is bound to say the inherent in this is the rather arrogant belief that prevails far too much among politicians–that everybody is naive but them. Volunteers don't take any more kindly to being exploited than anyone else. Do they really believe that we in SHELTER, and the people working so hard in the housing associations, are going to lightly stand by and allow ourselves to be exploited?

One of the questions raised in 1969 was about the number of problem families and poor families rehoused by SHELTER–type housing associations. This concern was shared by myself.

Until the rent rebate schemes became available, there were some families that a housing association, without massive injections of charitable money, just could not afford to re-house. Further, the re-housing of larger families remained a nightmare problem. And finally, the kind of highly-effective welfare help needed by families with multiple problems was tremendously time-consuming and therefore expensive, and again was something that was difficult for a housing association to do on any large scale.

I would say that up until now SHELTER has helped to rehouse problem families and poor families, proportionate to their numbers among the homeless. It's important to underline that last phrase, for it's wrong to assume that the only families that can become homeless are problem families—one must repeat again that the homeless are on the whole good, ordinary, low-income families who are just victims of acute housing stress.

Nevertheless, I have been questioning within SHELTER whether the time might not be coming when SHELTER should concentrate more and more on the more vulnerable groups, such as problem families and poor families, who always seem to miss out, no matter what is done.

What concerns me is that there is a small group of families who really do appear to be permanently on the bottom rung of the social ladder, and who, no matter what is done, always seem to be the losers.

Whilst it is possible to point to the most dreadful problems with the parents, some of whom just seem unable to discipline themselves to pay rent, and to others who have considerable social problems, one has to consider the children, and ask: "If it is thought that the children will be best off if they stay with their parents, it is not in society's interest to carry the parents, practically regardless, rather than see the family break-up?"

These are questions that SHELTER will have to be continually asking itself over the next few years.

Before moving on from the housing association operation, that has been such an essential part of SHELTER's rescue programme, there are one or two points that still concern me.

Firstly, I am deeply concerned about the national leadership of the movement. It seems to me that the voluntary housing movement, apart from rescuing families and properties, brings flexibilty, humanity, and all of the advantages of idealism into a field that has lacked idealism for far too long. It is vital that such qualities be retained, but there seems to me to be something of a gulf between the idealism at grassroots level, the independence and even militancy that exists there, and the leadership provided by organisations like the National Federation of Housing Societies, who negotiate with the authorities and are singularly ineffective in projecting that idealism and militancy.

SHELTER has endeavoured to offer some of that national leadership, but has no brief and is hardly welcomed by bureaucracy. Bureaucracy prefers to deal with bureaucracy, and the existence of the National Federation of Housing Societies and other establishment bodies must be a considerable relief to the Civil Service, who are able to duck meeting many of the most effective in the voluntary housing movement by dealing with these quasi-governmental bodies.

Secondly, I don't think the movement is sufficiently conscious of the need to hand over to another generation in good time. Far too many movements die because people die while still holding the key offices, their contribution in the latter years often being to hold back the same operation they once moved forwards. Often when the movement is handed over to a fresh generation, it is with grudging reluctance and in such a way that the new generation is frustrated by its inability to effect change.

Anyone who goes to the A.G.M. of the National Federation of Housing Socieites will not be inspired by the age or background of many of the people there, or many of the views expressed.

Finally, I've already referred to the reluctance of the voluntary housing movement to involve the homeless in its own activities. The belief that there is a management class, and a class of tenants and "ne'er the twain shall meet" still exists among many people in the voluntary housing movement.

The effect of all this is that the housing association movement has to a degree broken up, and around

SHELTER has congregated a small group of fast-moving housing associations, that have tended to treat the National Federation as largely irrelevant, and formed their own negotiating body in London, for instance, achieving most of the advantages that housing associations now have in the city.

There are discouraging signs that the tendency seems to be to move towards more consolidation at the top, and closer integration with the establishment. In my view this is something to be resisted.

Readers may be surprised at the scope of the political problems that housing associations too, have to face. But this movement does not ask that its importance be taken for granted and is more than able to stand up for itself. If the next two or three years are a somewhat traumatic experience, it is merely the price the movement will be paying for its own effectiveness, and there is no doubt in my mind that it is a bright ray of hope for the homeless at a time when the outlook has been distinctly gloomy.

For myself, and SHELTER, I cannot pay adequate tribute to the housing associations that have been our partners in this rescue operation. Without the money we raise they might not have been effective, but without them, our money would have had no meaning.

Neighbourhood Action Project

October 9, 1968

"Liverpool 8, the twilight zone of multi-occupied houses near to the city centre of Liverpool, is to be the scene for one of the most ambitious housing and neighbourhood projects ever to be undertaken by volunteers in a British city. The project–Liverpool SNAP (SHELTER *Neighbourhood Action Project)– was announced today after approval in principle by the Liverpool City Council."*

In 1968 and 1969 I became increasingly concerned about the problem of urban decay in Britain, and what could be done to arrest the tendency to allow area after area to go downhill until a bulldozer was the only answer.

Further, I was somewhat concerned about the "single-purchase" housing association approach, involving the purchase of one house here, and another house there. This can lead to an area looking like a patchwork quilt–some bright spots, some dull spots: some well-preserved and rehabilited houses, some slums: and create isolated cells that do nothing to preserve the community spirit.

We had been arguing that housing was essential to creative and happy family life, but it seemed to me that equally essential must be a practical and healthy environment, and if possible a creative and well-balanced community.

And so I put up a proposal to the Trustees that we should move over to the idea of not rehabilitating one house here, and another there, but entire areas, where the emphasis was as much on the rehabilitation of housing as on charitable help for the people. We would encourage the concept of helping people to help themselves, by creating situations where they would participate far more in the planning and carrying out of the projects and in the running of housing associations and other activities. We would link housing with community and environmental activities. We would link re-housing with housing aid and advice services, so that people could see that it was within their capacity to widen the range of choice for themselves and their families;

In my speech to the SHELTER Rally in 1969 I said:

> **"We hope to encourage local authorities and housing associations to form coalitions to carry out imaginative projects to alter the face of whole communities. Imagine what that means: no longer would a district be allowed to decay until it has to be**

torn down. We can rehabilitate this district working with the local authorities, owner/occupiers, property owners, residents and community associations. The community itself will not be lost and replaced at the cost of the community spirit that will never be recovered. We will stop the reduction in housing because of rebuilding at a lower destiny.

"I want to underline, too, that this is not abandoning the rescue operation but is the most effective way of helping the homeless as we define them. And it is rescue combined with experiment, and that experiment if a success will become a form of pressure in itself by creating a demand for more like it.

"This could lead to more families getting more homes in a more stable community than could be achieved in any other way. This links housing with environment and community. It challenges old concepts and could be SHELTER's greatest historical contribution to social change in this country."

And so it was decided to carry out an experimental scheme over three years, and Liverpool City Council agreed that the Granby triangle, a triangular group of roughly 740 houses in Liverpool 8, could be the site of the experiment.

Again, an understanding of the work of SNAP requires some knowledge of Liverpool 8. A local councillor, writing in the SHELTER newspaper, described its growing problems in this way:

"What of the future? What of the people? The prospect is dark. The city's unbelievable burden of condemned housing means that the claims of this area rank pitifully low in the batting order for attention. Ten years, fifteen, who knows how long, must pass before clearance can even be considered. And most dismaying of all, in that ten years, the houses must be allowed to degenerate to a level of squalor which will convince the "Powers That Be" that this is a slum.

Clearance Orders apply to slums, not to gallantly maintained dwellings, where proud people have papered over the cracks to keep up at least the appearance of decency. "We kept our place decent." they say. " and so we will never be rehoused."

What will this once sturdy community undergo in that ten years? What degradation of standards, what frittering away of moral conviction, what disintegration of hope must be endured before the whole place can be swept clear?

And what will be lost in the process? In spite of all the wear and tear of the past half century–or rather because of it–this is a living community still. Kill it off, and we destroy a web of loyalty and tradition, custom and habit, which it will take long years to re-create. These are people who have taken the first steps towards the art of how to live in a big city. Out of harsh experience they have already acquired the basic social skills of that community way of life which is so earnestly discussed at conferences. They have for that reason much to give. Are we prepared to benefit by their experience, to believe that these modest citizens can in fact teach us all a lesson?

There is one ray of brilliant hope in this dark scene. Not for nothing was this community founded on an aspiration for self-improvement! Even at this late stage there remains a determination to fight back, a conviction that the downward drift can be halted, a deep yearning to "get back to normal". They don't know how, but they are prepared to try.

One thing they do know, they cannot cope single-handed. With all the values of self-sufficiency and independence which their lives embody, they are in desperate need of help. If they are to be enabled to escape the fate which threatens them, they must be given the benefit of every modern resources. Give us

half a chance, they say, and we can manage. They have already set about providing their half of that chance: an active Community Council, groups of residents in street meetings, a Traders Association and an all too rare getting-together of School Managers and Head Teachers. Expectantly they wait . . . for our half of their chance to materialise.".

Des McConaghy, the volatile planner and dynamic personality who was appointed as Director of SNAP, describes its overall role as "the comprehensive, social, physical, and economic rehabilitation of a deteriorating residental area: to raise the living and environmental standards of residents and develop a process by which people can participate and meet their own needs more fruitfully."

An old police station was converted into the SNAP office and opened in July, 1969, and direct contact established with local authority offices dealing with housing, town planning, public health, open space, recreation, highways, welfare, water and other services, legal matters and finance.

The initial cynicism in the area was quickly overcome, and in July, 1969 there were 45 residents' meetings–three mass meetings, 17 street group meetings, and 25 meetings of residents' task forces dealing with such objects as housing, services, traffic and landscaping, education and recreation, crime and vandalism, and the advice centre itself.

Exhibitions were set up, a residents news sheet was introduced and a distribution of information on grants, mortgages, applications for improvement in contract procedure began. The show houses have been open for public inspection (the main one being opened by Ken Dodd) and a meeting hall was built.

The area was surveyed and from this it was established

that three-quarters of all households lacked at least one basic amenity, and almost one third lacked the sole use of any basic amenity.

People in 552 households were interviewed as part of a survey, providing an overall response of 71.9%.

This established that a high proportion were non-manual workers and the average earnings were about £12 a week. 65% of all respondents said they liked their house and thought it could be improved, the main demands being repairs to the inside of the house, and the roof, and installation of hot water, inside w.c.s and baths.

The report concluded that more people liked the area than disliked it, and most of the difficulties could be dealt with by improved services, public cleansing, new back alleys and improved roads, pavements and lighting.

Although a massive loss of confidence had arisen from a long history of poor public and private maintenance, and from the decline of services and general blight, the people living there became quickly excited at the idea of improving the area, and began to investigate the opportunities of the 1969 Housing Act with imagination, spirit, and tenacity. All of this is reflected in one highly impressive fact: in 1968 one improvement grant was paid in the area: over the past 14 years, an average of three improvement grants were paid: yet in the first six months of the SNAP operation, 150 applications were made for improvement grants. This not only shows the willingness of people in an area like this to participate in the improvement of an area, when their faith is restored, but the importance of having an advisory centre among them.

At the time of writing the report that is required, under Section 28 of the Housing Act 1969, has been submitted by the SNAP team to the Council, and as soon as the area is named as a general Improvement Area, the special subsidies and grants made possible by the Housing Act will come into effect.

Up to now SNAP has achieved remarkable results, thanks to the incredibly hard work of Des McConaghy, Dave Wilkinson, and the other workers in the SNAP centre.

But this is where the coalition comes in, for now the local authority has to play its part, in making available the services and the manpower that will be essential to a major rehabilitation scheme. The aim of SHELTER at the beginning was to get a team together and begin planning nearly a year before the White Paper, "Old Houses into New Homes" became an Act, and thus create a shop window for the whole concept–if you like put flesh and blood on the bones of legislation.

SHELTER has never claimed to have invented the concept of neighbourhood rehabilitation. Nor has it said it was the only one that could do it. But it wanted to boost the concept of coalitions involving the maximum number of people–off the streets, from organisations, and from local authorities–and it is this community participation that is its unique feature.

It is best reflected in the SNAP news, the project newspaper that is circulated monthly to all people within the SNAP map:

Snap News –August 1969

Ideas

Miss S. proposes that public telephone kiosks should be put outside a dwellinghouse and the G.P.O. should install, free of rent, a telephone in the house so that the kiosk can be supervised. Brilliant!

Mr. N. is saving space with a shower unit rather than a bath. He has given us some good tips. Thanks, too, to a lady who brought in details of a breakfast table and benches that fold neatly into a wall unit. And another fantastic idea was the man who wanted to make his cellar into a bathroom and so save a bedroom.

Frankly we don't think this will work–but not to worry–it's your ideas we want. Miss P. is keen that the back alleys are lit, but let's just note this until we have got a complete answer to those horrible "backs'. Suppose everyone had a bigger yard by getting rid of the alleys? This was another good idea, but leaves us with the problem of refuse disposal. We are looking at every answer, including paper sacks and special disposal units.

Don't forget we'll be coming to each house in September to see you, and in the meantime you should be discussing and thinking about it, making notes of anything that concerns you.

Street Meetings

Residents of Cawdor and Ponsonby Streets came out on July 20 to air their problems and ideas for improvement. Kerb crawling traffic is the burning issue, and the group has collected 128 signatures petitioning the corporation to stop motor cars entering these two streets from Mulgrave Street.

Did you know that an 11 seater mini-bus was available seven days a week for any trips, children's and old peoples' outings etc. It's fully insured and free–all you need is a responsible driver and payment of petrol.

Snap News–September 1969

More Ideas

Mr Whittaker says some front rooms aren't used, and recommends that people use the back living room as a dining kitchen and the back kitchen as a bathroom. This good idea has been explored on drawings by the SHAC team and can be seen in the project office. Mrs. Richardson reckons that cellars could be converted into attractive playrooms. Mrs. Williams

says that the reconstruction of roads in the improvement of the environment should allow for gardens at the front of the houses. Mr. C has some more ideas about space-saving bath arrangements—this time, it's a bath and shower unit combined, measuring only three feet by three feet.
The idea about telephone supervision in the first newsheet has been picked up by the local newspaper.

News
Mrs. Richardson in Cawdor Street may be the first person in Liverpool to have details of her house improvement worked out by computer.
We've arranged a bus trip to see the rehabilitation of houses at Old Skelmersdale.

Snap News—September 1969

It's Survey Time
Now we're coming to most houses in the area. The pilot study is already running. This is your survey and you need this information to support your proposals for the improvement of your houses.

News
Littlewoods, the pools people are letting us use their computer for the processing of information. Public Health Inspectors are in the area helping us collect information about the improvement of property. Don't worry—it doesn't mean the houses are coming down.
Peter Walker, Shadow Minister of Housing, carried out his own survey of the SNAP area. Everyone he spoke to knew about the project and said they were supporting it. A pretty good indication of your splendid efforts in attending street meetings, reading the news sheets etc.

Ideas

Mrs. Cassidy wants the Corporation to leave large containers on derelict sites at useful position on certain days each month for the collection of large items of rubbish. We could throw out everything we don't want and organise "massive clear-ups" on these days.

Mrs. Fitzgerald writes: "We spoke to some children throwing down papers. 'Pick that up' said my husband sternly, and added jocularly 'Keep britain Tidy'. Came the reply: 'This isn't Britain–it's Liverpool.'"

Snap News–November 1969

It's election time

On October 28 about 200 residents of SNAP met in the School Hall and decided to hold an election to find three residents to represent the area on the Committee of SNAP.

The Council is also nominating three members. If you want to be a candidate for the SNAP election, send your name in now.

Task forces are starting work, and arrangements are being made for building a Community Council Meeting Hall by the SNAP office. Volunteers required this weekend to dig out the sub-soil before the contractor puts in his slab.

Dave Wilkinson is finalising details for your show houses. Watch out for the grand openings.

Snap News–November 1969

Meet your candidates for the election–Mr. Hughes from Kens Street has lived in the area all his life and wants SNAP to succeed. "He wants to work for more law enforcement by the police to get rid of the nuisance of kerby crawling, and wants SNAP to keep on at the Corporation for telephones, frequent cleaning of the streets. "There is no use in improving the houses if it still is a bad area".

Mrs. Martha Igbinovia lives in Beaconsfield and is a young housewife with two children. She was born in the area and thinks there is a lot wrong with it and SNAP can help. She attends meetings of the task forces on housing and education and says: "SNAP must not forget the problems of the young and the old. With two young children I want to work hard to improve the schools and solve the lack of play areas. I have no hesitation in standing up for the area. I want to live here, but it must be fit to bring up a family in."

Mrs. Josephine Navji is standing because "It's difficult to get insurance for shops, streets are dirty, and kerb crawling is a real nuisance. Law and order must be enforced by the police and the residents. Then the people will have the incentive to do up their property and the breaking and entering problem will decline.

Mr. O'Grady from Jermyn Street was first to come forward as a candidate. He's retired but worked in the building trade. He has lived here most of his life and in on our housing task force.

Mr. Venables from Eversley Street is well-known at SNAP. He knows what people want and will do his best on the Committee for them.

Bert Sutherland has lived for 37 years in Ponsonby Street. I've seen the area going down for many years and I think it's high time we came forward and helped to bring this area back to what it was. To do this we need all your help. I am sure we can do just that now SNAP is here to help us get the improvements we badly need. I am already on two of

the task forces for services and vice vandalism. I'm also on the Princes Park and Granby Committee Council, so if you think I'm the right man for the job, vote for me on Sunday."
A mobile voting van will call at each street equipped with a lound speaker during Sunday. Also SNAP offices will be open if the van is in your street at the wrong time. Voting slips will be available and you can vote for three out of the six canditates.

Snap News–December 1969

Mrs. Hughes, Martha Igbinovia and Bert Sutherland have been elected. They represent you and are concerned about your concerns. Tell them what you think.
By the way the 891 votes cast were more than for the local authority elections.

Free Legal Advice
SNAP is providing free landlord-tenant, housing, and dwelling–improvement advice. Now we need to expand, and in the prefab there is going to be a full free legal advice service, manned by qualified, experienced solicitors. It will help you on land law, family law, tenant law, estate law, prostitution nuisance–you name it. And it's in the Granby area–for Granby residents. In fact many more solicitors have volunteered for the rota than will be needed–so the service will be good. Remember: Wednesday evenings at SNAP 7 p.m.–9 p.m.

Kerb Crawling
This is being tackled by the Residents Crime Task. It is a modern nuisance, no really efficient legal means exists yet to counter it. But police can take action

under a local byelaw against "offensive behaviour". What they want is good evidence. Merely for a man to follow a woman in a car is nothing as evidence in a court of law. Take down the registration number, a description of the driver, and the words or acts that are offensive. Ring the police, using if necessary SNAP's 24 hour phone, and they will take a statement from you and interview the driver and take the matter as far as they can. The police have rarely been approached. They want you to know they are prepared to act and if we get a few convictions and they are given publicity without mentioning the name of the woman involved, this is the best deterrent possible.

Battle of the Backs!

The battle of what to do about the backs rages one. Some residents seem to favour widening the backs, others favour widening the yards and doing away with the alleys and are at present getting the SNAP team to design an attractive vandal-proof paper sack container for the street to solve the refuse problem. What do you think?

Tree Pruning Demonstration

Are the trees going to be looked after? Yes, and the Corporation will demonstrate how they can be controlled and pruned in Arundel Street on Tuesday.

Snap News–January 1970

The total number of improved units of accommodation being processed is 229.

A mass meeting is planned for January 27 to talk about the task forces of residents proposed for the area–one way streets, blocking of streets, closing of one end of Granby Street, new pedestrian crossing new community centres, youth club and bar, a pub in Granby Street, stronger social law against kerb crawlers, a parent/teacher association–all these and more can be discussed and your vote is essential.

Welfare Jungle
SNAP is broadening its information service to cover things like consumer rights, your relationship with the welfare state, with the W.E.A. we are organising talks in our community hut on the administration of an information centre, the work of the welfare department, the landlord and tenant, work of the Rent Officer, work of the Rent Tribunal, and the probation service. Also a talk on National Insurance supplementary benefits and allowances.

Snap News–Improvement Special

The SNAP report has gone to the Corpy.
At last our report can go to the City Corporation, containing your proposals and the costs for making SNAP a general improvement area under the 1969 Housing Act. The proposals can be seen at an exhibition over Easter Weekend and discussed at a mass meeting of residents of SNAP on April 2.
HERE'S THE CHALLENGE:
now, LET'S SEE THE CHANGE!
(P.S. Ken Dodd is opening our SNAP show houses on April 8. No Kidding. So bring your tickling stick!)

Housing Aid and Advice

One cannot begin to talk about the concept of housing aid and advice without referring to Eamonn Casey.

Eamonn came from Ireland in 1960 at the age of 33, to be Chaplain to Irish immigrants in Slough. Nine years later he returned to Ireland as Bishop of Kerry, having made the name of Casey a legend in the world of voluntary housing. It's extraordinary how few people outside of voluntary housing know about Casey, but this is the key to his outstanding quality, a humility that has caused him to sledge-hammer his personality into the depths of the movement, rather than to project himself out in front.

Nevertheless, he has been a chairman of SHELTER, on the Council of the National Federation of Housing Societies, founder-director of the Catholic Housing Aid Society and the Family Housing Association, a director of the British Churches Housing Trust, and a member of the Commission for Social Welfare.

He was born one of ten children, five boys and five girls, of a tough and shrewd businessman who only retired a couple of years ago at 78.

Eamonn Casey was ordained as a curate to the City of Limerick in 1951 and for four years taught religion to 14–18 year olds at the City Vocational School. In 1955 he was moved to a parish enclosing roughly 2,000 people and in addition to all of the duties of a priest was chaplin to an orphanage, a hospital, a prison, and an asylum, as well as organising a boys' club, a mixed youth club, four Scout troops, and a Young Christian Workers group.

Typical of Eamonn Casey is the story of the waste paper company.

In order to raise money for a new college, he and a group of volunteers set to collect waste paper for pulping. A local company agreed to take all the paper they provided, and for five years this worked well. Then the company cut its price, but still they continued to work and accept the reduced rate. Shortly after the Company suddenly moved out, almost overnight. Seven of their staff, male and female, were left unemployed. At this point when most people would have dropped the whole idea, Eamonn Casey hired the old company staff, kept them in their jobs, bought his own transport, baling machines, and the other equipment, and re-started the business, running it himself at a profit.

Under different management, the business still exists today.

When he came to Slough he found 300 factories and a steady demand for both male and female labour, but a desperate need for housing. He set up a lodgings' bureau and a savings scheme designed to help people to buy their own homes. As all the investors in this scheme saved with the same bank, it in turn agreed to lend small amounts to the customers, and thereby aid them with a deposit on the house. In his first year he helped 19 families to buy a home.

But the savings scheme was not in itself an answer to the problem. Eamonn Casey found many people living in slums, paying high rents, and finding it impossible to save at all. He decided the housing association concept of buying houses, converting them into decent flats, and then letting them to the families at realistic rents was the answer and came together with some people who were forming a Catholic Housing Aid Society. He became its first Director, and based it on the centre he had run in Slough–aiding people to purchase their own homes, rehousing badly house families in SHAC flats, and encouraging single people to save.

Over the years additional schemes were formed and slowly the whole concept of housing aid and advisory services was pioneered.

Soon the Catholic Housing Aid Society centre in Holland Road, Shepherds Bush, became the biggest voluntary centre of its kind, providing the most comprehensive service. Eamonn Casey insisted that it helped people regardless of race or religion, and so although it carried the name "Catholic" it helped people of all religions.

Its reputation grew, and with it the reputation of Eamonn Casey. It began branches throughout the country and by 1970 had started 63. By then the centre was dealing with nearly 80 enquiries a week, and attracting the attention of everybody concerned with tackling the housing problem.

Professor David Donnison wrote a paper on housing aid and advice, basing it on what he had learned from Eamonn Casey, and the Seabohm Committee recommended that it was a concept that should be furthered in every local authority area in the country. Then a sub-committee set up by the Ministry to look into local authority housing also came out for the concept, and Eamonn Casey's brainchild had become regarded by most as an essential part of the British housing scene.

SHELTER saw housing aid and advisory centres not as an alternative to housing associations, or local authority services, but rather as an essential adjunct to them, making them both all the more effective.

So it was decided to devote 6 per cent of SHELTER's income to housing aid, and to open a major experiment in housing aid in London.

This was to be the SHELTER Housing Aid Centre, and the Catholic Housing Aid Society agreed to shut down its own London headquarters, and help to provide the manpower to run the new one.

SHAC was going to cost well over £100,000 a year to run, but the importance of the experiment was recognised by a number of Trusts and Foundations, and the Joseph Rowntree Memorial Trust and the Calouste Gulbenkian Foundation each agreed to pay £15,000 a year for three years, and the Barrow and Geraldine Cadbury Trust another £10,000.

One should emphasise that this is not to pay for administration in the usual sense, but for the complete cost of the provision of a service.

Once again SHELTER delegated responsibility and an entirely separate board of Trustees and staff took over the running of the Centre, under the direction of Father Paul

Byrne, who had run the Family Housing Association and the Catholic Housing Aid Society in Birmingham, and who had become Eamonn Casey's successor when he went back to Ireland.

Paul had wide experience of practical housing problems, determination and intelligence. Inexperienced in running a human machine of this kind, he nevertheless faced the problem with considerable courage, apparently undaunted by the problems it created.

The Centre was put into the Boltons, a particularly fashionable part of South Kensington. This may seem a strange address for a Centre to help the homeless in but that is precisely why it was put there. We didn't want the Centre to be in a twilight zone or problem area–like, say North Kensington–for then it would have quickly become associated with that area, and come to be seen by people to be only helping families in that area.

We wanted any homeless family in London to feel free to go to SHAC.

The existence of a housing advisory and aid centre recognises that some peoples' problems can be helped by advice alone, and others need advice with some help towards their own solution. It is the specific help that is, in fact, housing aid.

SHAC is envisaged as what the Americans call a "one-call office". It's geared to deal with a family's housing problem, not by having them shot around from one agency to another becoming more and more discouraged and more and more hopeless, but by bringing the family in once, to have them present their case to a trained interviewer. The case is then assessed, and one or other of the solutions available pursued.

The Centre employs over 40 full-time staff, trained and experienced in social work, social administration, the law, accountancy, housing management, and the mortgage and building society fields.

The standard of the interviewing is particularly high, the expert being Ted Wade, a man who combines firmness with kindness, and has probably more experience in interviewing homeless families than anybody else in the country. One day we worked out that he had probably interviewed 12,000 families. All of the work Ted has done, both for the Catholic Housing Aid Society and SHELTER working full-time, has been voluntary.

Behind the team of full-time professionals lie a considerable number of trained voluntary interviewers.

SHAC works on the basis that the ideal solution to a family's problem is to buy a home of their own. Paul Byrne tells me:

> **"Some people can do this merely by our giving them advice and by explaining what a mortgage is, how to go about getting a mortgage, what savings they need, the precise mortgage they as a family will get, by giving our advice on building societies, banks, and estate agents. The family can then leave us, go away, and buy a house. But usually the whole question of advice spills over into the need for aid, whether the aid be motivation towards savings in or the setting up of a very definite saving system, with a specific bank and a specific building society tailored to their individual needs. The aid might, for instance, take the form of a bank loan which we would recommend when the family had shown by their savings that they could carry this together with their mortgage repayments for a year or two.**
>
> **"Much of this sort of advisory and aid work towards house purchase is, of course done with the young people before marriage, in the short-term with engaged couples, and in the long-term with talks to schools."**

For instance, one young couple came to SHAC some time before their marriage, having already begun to save with a building society through a bank. SHAC discovered that this building society would not accept the fiancee's wages for mortgage purposes because she did not have a profession, and introduced the couple to a society which would take both the wages into account at the time of the marriage. His own bank was unwilling to advance them a loan if he needed to top up the deposit, so again SHAC was able to introduce him to a bank which would. They were able to buy a house in Surrey and are paying £5,275 for it. In fact, they didn't need to use the building society since SHAC helped them to get a loan of £4,970 from the G.L.C.

It's possible that family would have bought its home. It's also possible that without expert advice it might have failed.

It is amazing how many families can be helped one way or another to buy a home. One third of the families that went to SHAC in its first two months are now being helped to buy their own home.

Unfortunately, often the most desperate families could never think of buying a home, for the average industrial wage is far from the average mortgage repayment. Paul Byrne says:

> **"The first solution we look for is moving the family out of London altogether. A whole department specialises in knowing the housing situation and employment position in other parts of England. Good interviewing is essential, the family that lives in bad housing has to realise that there is civilization beyond Luton and that houses may be as little as half the price there, and that there is a new life waiting for them and for their children in places like Halifax, where we've got a full time official working on the integration of families."**

Take the case of Mr. and Mrs. G., who had two very young children and were living in one room in the sister's house, where they should not have been anyway since the sister had bought her house on a council mortgage. Family tensions arose and they were asked to move out within a week. SHAC got them into emergency housing until such time as they could find a council house in Halifax, where they are now happily settled, and the husband is working in his old job as a bus conductor.

In the first two months, SHAC encouraged 127 families to plan the move out of London.

When SHELTER stepped in this scheme was moving about one family a week out of London, and this is being increased to one a day, and we hope many more.

The SHAC branches play an invaluable role here, finding the home, schooling, and employment for the families, and often the mortgage too.

I remember another family, the M family, living in a damp, overcrowded flat at a rent of £4 a week with an income of £17. They didn't have a toilet ot a kitchen of their own. Now they live in Nottingham in a three-bedroomed house with kitchen, toilet and bathroom, which they bought for £1,300 repaying a mortgage at £13.10.0. a month. The husband now earns £18 a week. In this case we paid the deposit, but normally the family saves up the money to pay for this.

The toughest department to work in in SHAC is the London Referral Department, whose job it is to find private rented housing, council housing, or housing association flats for families that have to rent.

Such a family were Mr. and Mrs. A., and their three children, who came to SHAC on the point of eviction. Their problem was so urgent it went to the Emergency Department, who were able to refer them to a Borough Welfare Officer who put them in emergency accomodation. But the Welfare Department was unable to have them housed immediately by the council, although it found out the council would rehouse them in a few years time. SHAC then conferred with the Family Housing Association, with whom it works particularly closely. They had negotiated a considerable amount of short life property out of the G.L.C., and so Mr. and Mrs. A. were rehoused there, with the Council giving a guarantee that at the end of the life of that property they would give Mr. and Mrs. A. a permanent council home.

SHAC is now working particularly closely with the SHELTER-backed housing associations in London, and taking over some of the interviewing for them, in return for a share of the accomodation they create.

In three months it interviewed over 1,000 families, and this gives some indication of the problem that exists.

It could be that local authorities will show themselves able to run housing advisory centres in such a way that voluntary centres will be unnecessary, but this can't be properly assessed unless there is one highly-effective voluntary centre to act as a bisis for comparison, and that is why SHAC is such an important experiment.

Local authorities will, in any event, restrict their housing advisory centres to their own local authority areas, and we felt there was a need for a central agency, both to help the family that was being shunted from borough to borough, or to act as an outside adviser if a family feels it is getting a rough deal.

Because SHAC will be drawing information on the extent and type of homelessness that exists in every part of London, it will also act as a barometer of the problem.

In addition to bringing hope to many families, it will unquestionably turn the searchlight on the dark corners of London where so many families live in misery and squalor with no firm help or advice, and turn the searchlight on any gaps in the system. Working effectively with the authorities, and we hope accepted as a help to them, it will also be a well-intentioned critic of their faults.

Not that SHAC will be able to avoid making its own mistakes. It's an experiment and it's new. Somebody has to take the risks, and we are prepared to. It won't be infallible. We've no doubt, too, that SHAC will fail many families. In doing so, SHAC will suffer with the families. But as time goes by, we hope it will be able to reduce the number day by day, both by increasing its own efficiency and range of contacts and also by creating more centres of its kind to deal with problems in different localities, both in London and other parts of the country.

In the meantime, SHELTER is working to promote the concept of housing advice and housing aid and at least one of the major political parties, the Conservatives, are committed to setting up a chain throughout the country.

Once again it has to be emphasised that housing aid and advisory centres may assume different characters according to who runs them, and where they are run.

SHAC should not be regarded as the only kind of housing aid centre necessary. All sorts of tenants' rights centres, and residence centres should be encouraged.

The SNAP advisory centre contrasts sharply with the SHELTER Housing Aid Centre in London, but the SNAP centre is also a formidable one.

One of the SNAP secrets is that several of its team worked for the local authority, and know how to deal with it. For instance, many families don't know how to present their case to the council. Mr. and Mrs. Gordon had for months and months been writing to Liverpool housing officials saying they wanted to leave their bad housing and move into a council falt, but always received refusals, if they received a reply at all. Then they went to the SNAP advice centre, and one of the team typed out a letter for them to sign. It went like this:

> **Dear Sir,**
>
> **My husband and I are housing applicants in the IF stream. We have only five points. In our present accomodation (two rooms for which we pay £4 per week) we have no bathroom and a w.c. is**

unusuable–we have to go across the road to a friend's house for this purpose. In addition, the noise from other residents in this multi-occupied house means that my husband is unable to sleep properly, which is affecting his work.

Our attempts to find better accomodation have met with no success, so I am writing to ask if we may be considered for a "prolonged vacancy" in one of the multi-storey blocks, preferably in Liverpool 8 or 7. We are both earning and able to pay the necessary rent. We would be quite willing to take on a three bedroomed flat, as we understand these are more readily available.

We look forward hopefully to your reply.

Yours faithfully."

Two weeks later the family was in a three-bedroomed council flat.

The Belfast operation

December 1, 1969 "Families made homeless during the Belfast riots are to be offered temporary homes by SHELTER, the National Campaign for the Homeless. "Mr. Des Wilson, Director of SHELTER, flew unannounced to Belfast at the weekend and apparently gave the Northern Ireland authorities a brisk ultimatum: to cut red tape and accept £200,000 of housing within 48 hours, or face the political uproar which would result if they lost the chance of rehousing 100 families immediately."

Alec Greenhalgh, The Guardian, December 1, 1969.

SHELTER's operation in Northern Ireland was hardly a world-shattering event, but in its daring and in its speed it did illustrate what a campaign that has built-in flexibility and "guts" can do when an opportunity arises.

The "troubles" in Northern Ireland created a new breed of homeless family–families literally afraid to return to their homes.

Jo Connelly, slight, softly-spoken, bespectacled, mild and essentially a family man told me that the strain of living "near the front"—the Falls Road—had been beginning to tell and so on the night of August 15 he took to sleeping pills. He slept through a riot, and woke to find houses burning in the street, and, in his own words "all hell let loose."

The next day, Joe, who is father of six children, got the message: "Get out—or else." As he put it: "With six kids, who was going to stay around to find out what they meant?"

Another family that I met, the Sullivans, were burned out on the night of August 10. When the shooting began, they were forced to lie on the floor in a back room for protection. As the houses along the road blazed, they finally escaped, but when they returned to rescue their furniture they found the house had been ransacked and looted. "We lost everything. All we had left were the clothes we were wearing and the gas cooker. The house was in ruins."

So the Connellys and the Sullivans and many more ended up in intolerable prefabs on Beachmount, deeper into West Belfast. They had one living room, and in the case of Joe Connelly two bedrooms. The six children slept in one small, damp room, three girls in one bed, and the three boys sharing two bunks. The condensation was so bad that water streamed down the window forming pools on the window sill that eventually spilled over onto the carpet. Dampness crept up through the floor. There was no bathroom or toilet. The nearest toilet was on stilts and everybody was given a key to it, but in the dark it was no fun walking, practically knee-deep in mud, particularly if you were a child.

Caravans on the site were even worse, with one family of ten living in two small caravans. A coal fire burnt in one, and it was smoky, smelly and steamy. The doctor had been called five times in the last few weeks.

This was the situation, and although the Northern Ireland authorities had in some respects moved remarkably quickly, many, many families were faced with a grim Christmas.

This was the situation on Monday, November 24, when Desmond Plummer, leader of the Greater London Council, and Horace Cutler, Chairman of the Housing Committee, came for a working lunch with John Coward, John Willis, Cindy Barlow and myself at SHELTER.

After chatting about mutual problems for some time, Plummer said he had something to offer SHELTER: 500 mobile homes over two years. It turned out that the homes were high-standard, temporary houses, purpose-built by the G.L.C. to help with the decanting of slum clearance areas. The G.L.C. was running out of land, and finding that the cost of moving them was becoming prohibitive. They offered one hundred immediately–"You can have them today" and the rest over the next couple of years.

After Plummer and Cutler left, I put up the idea to my colleagues that we might offer them to the Northern Ireland authorities as emergency housing. A fast-moving operation could get at least some of them over for Christmas.

I contacted Des McConaghy of Liverpool SNAP, who has a number of contacts at national and local Government level in Northern Ireland, and he agreed to make some preliminary telephone calls.

The telephones buzzed for a couple of days as I firstly confirmed with the G.L.C. that the 100 homes could be made available quickly, and that we could use them anywhere in the U.K. Horace Cutler agreed to push the allocation through as an emergency item at his housing committee meeting on the Thursday afternoon, and in the meantime, Des McConaghy had persuaded the Minstry of

Dedvelopment in Northern Ireland to send over an expert to look at the homes on the Friday.

Throughout the week we built up the momentum for the operation, and on the Friday a representative of the Housing Division of the Ministry of Development arrived, and was shown around the homes, together with people from the G.L.C. Architect's office.

It soon became apparent that the houses were of sufficient quality, and two major problems remained: firstly, transporting them to Northern Ireland quickly; secondly, persuading the Northern Ireland authorities to pay the costs.

I rang David Owen, Under-Secretary for the Royal Navy, and asked him for an aircraft carrier. To my surprise he took the whole matter seriously, and after investigations said that the Navy could perhaps help out in an emergency. Fortunately, by then John Willis had found out that it was easier and quicker to take them up the M.1 and across the Irish Sea by ferry, and so we didn't need to bother David Owen any further.

Des McConaghy and I got into Belfast by the Sunday morning, and drove past soldiers with machine guns and walkie-talkies, past the so-called "peace line" of rolls of barbed wire, till we came to Beachmount, the site occupied by 50 caravans and 50 temporary houses. It was to be a day of frantic meetings, with the homeless on the sites, representatives of the Catholic community, and local officials, who turned up in a voluntary capacity to have talks about what could be done.

Everyone agreed that there was a need for more good-standard temporary housing.

The locals were somewhat sceptical about our ability to persuade the Ministry of Development to act quickly, and it was agreed that the only hope was to get Brian Faulkner, the Minister of Development, behind the scheme.

A meeting was fixed between myself and Mr. Faulkner for

half past ten on the Monday morning, and in order to build up the pressure on him stories were leaked to the Irish newspapers and to The Guardian about the offer.

The crucial day was the Monday, one week after Plummer and Cutler had originally made their offer of the homes. I made some diary notes for that day and they read:

> *"Woken up at 6.30 a.m. by the B.B.C. who wanted an interview for Today programme via the telephone, I talked with Jack de Manio, and a few minutes later heard it broadcast back. The newspapers were full of the story, with the main local newspaper making it their front page lead, and The Guardian giving it prominence. This publicity was in my view essential to the negotiation. By the time we got to a meeting with the Town Clerk and his advisers at Belfast City Corporation, there was little doubt in anyone's mind why we were there. They were fairly positive, and there was some discussion over sites, but general agreement that there was a need for the houses. Ulster Television rang to arrange an interview and said they had already telephoned Stormont and found Brian Faulkner reasonably positive about a television appearance. This suggested that he was already fairly committed to the idea of taking the houses. By the time we arrived at Stormont we judged the atmosphere was on our side, but Faulkner kept us waiting for about thirty minutes. By the time I was hauled in he was surrounded by his own officials, representatives of the Northern Ireland Housing Trust, and the Belfast Corporation. They went over basic questions about the situation once more, one of the main points being the price. I laid down four conditions: the homes were to be used as quickly as possible to help families in emergency circumstances and all efforts were to be made to get the families in by Christmas; they were to be regarded as temporary*

and should not prejudice in any way the provision of good standard permanent housing; the Northern Ireland authorities must meet the costs involved—about £1200 per house for transport and installation; proper arrangements must be made for maintenance of the housing and services. There is a slight brush with Faulkner over the radio broadcast in the morning and The Guardian story. Faulkner seemed fairly determined to keep me in my place, but I didn't much care what he said, as long as the houses were accepted. It was finally agreed that they should take 50 houses immediately and attempt to install them by Christmas and that we would hold another 50 in reserve for them."

In the meantime, John Willis had been performing miracles in lining up the transport of the mobile homes. The first of the shipment left London on December 9, having been picked up by crane from a site in Battersea, put on giant transporters and sent to Preston, from where they were shipped to Northern Ireland.

Two homes left London each day and 25 families were actually in their homes by Christmas.

It was decided that I should fly over on December 22 to see the families in their homes, and also to see the Ministry of Development about their option on a further 50.

Whether it was coincidence, or whether the Belfast authorities didn't want a repeat of the campaign that led to their acceptance of the first 50, I don't know, but a telegram arrived just before my departure from London to say that they were accepting the second 50 homes.

This was particularly encouraging, for by now the first homes had arrived in Belfast, and we took this to be an expression of satisfaction with them.

From SHELTER's point of view this had all made for a most exciting Christmas. It was heart-warming to see the families preparing to spend Christmas in much more comfortable conditions than they had dreamt would be possible. It was also exciting to think that we had been capable of pulling off a quite remarkable operation in only 22 days. In all this teamwork had been the key, and the two heroes of the exercise were John Willis, who was responsible for getting the homes over there, and Des McConaghy, who did most of the negotiating with the Northern Ireland officials to make the success possible.

TEN

"Where, after all, do universal human rights begin? In small places close to home–so close and so small that they cannot be seen on any map of the world. They are the world of the individual person: the neighbourhood he lives in; the school or college he attends; the factory, farm or office where he works. Such are the places where every man, woman and child seeks equal justice, equal opportunity, equal dignity without discrimination. Unless these rights have meaning there, they have little meaning anywhere. Without concerted citizen action to uphold them close to home, we shall look in vain for progress in the larger world."

–Eleanor Roosevelt

THE SHELTER STORY (3): PRESSURE

When we speak of pressure groups we tend to think of groups championing the cause of the under-privileged, or the socially unworthy. Yet such pressure groups are often competing with even more powerful groups working for even more powerful interests. Thus, when priorities are decided, the voice of the minority is often muted, if not drowned, by the lobbies of the majority, clinging often to the status quo.

Not only are the minorities out-gunned in the quantity of their protest, but also in the quality. In a society monopolized by a well-educated elite, governed by restrictive provisions and bureaucracy-ridden institutions, conditioned by an enormously influential communcations industry, and dictated to through a mass of fresh and complex legislation, the poor are made all the more powerless by the side-effects of poverty-prominent being lack of expertise.

So the first thing to say about pressure activities is that they are by no means restricted to the poor.

Pressure groups for the underprivileged or unprotected fall into a number of categories—they can be run by a group on its own behalf, as is the case with the Disablement Incomes Group, or can be run by a privileged class on behalf of an under-privileged class, as is the case with the Child Poverty Action Group.

Pressure groups can be fighting for a small minority group, as does the Gipsy Council, or on behalf of everybody, as is the case with the National Council for Civil Liberties.

They can be fighting on national lines, or at local level, and seeking legislative change, or just a more humanitarian approach to a specific problem.

And some, like SHELTER, combine their pressure activities with rescue. In this way each enhances the other, and also to a small degree inhibits the other, but this kind of pressure group is perhaps all the more influential for the balance it has to keep.

Before undertaking pressure activities, SHELTER had to ask itself a number of questions:

Should it campaign at national or local level?

Who should be the targets of pressure: society as a whole, or its administrators?

What should the nature of its pressure activities be?

Surprisingly, considering the size and scope of the

housing problem, there was no pressure group for the homeless on a national basis. The Child Poverty Action Group had spoken out from time to time on behalf of the homeless, and there had been occasional local pressure activities in different parts of the country, but this was all.

There were so many different aspects of the housing problem that one would like to have got one's teeth into: the remaining problems of insecurity, the inhumanities of the authorities towards the emergency homeless . . . indeed, it would take pages to list them.

But SHELTER decided that greater priority for housing, best reflected in an increased percentage of the G.N.P. should be the main aim of its pressure activities.

Taking the view that its pressure campaign would need to be sustained over a number of years, SHELTER believed that it was best to hold back pressure on specific aspects of housing policy, and on local issues, until a powerful attempt had been made to get more money into housing.

As I told the SHELTER Rally in 1970:

"When that point is made, and let's not kid ourselves we've made it yet, we can involve ourselves more fully in wider issues, but at present by debating specific policies or specific items of other expenditure that might be cut, we will only confuse our message and divide our audience.

"Up to now we've resisted, as far as possible, getting involved in two debates: firstly, on specific housing policies; and secondly, on where the additional money should come from.

"Clearly this is the policy that we must keep under constant review but I believe that in an election year, specially, it is the correct one."

Having taken the decision that the obtaining of greater social priority for housing must be our number one objective, we took a second decision that we would concentrate our pressure on society as a whole, in order to build up public opinion on the politicians of all parties.

And so SHELTER's campaign in its first three years was concentrated on establishing the extent of the housing problem, sustaining a sense of public urgency about housing, and countering any propoganda issued by the authorities that might lead to complacency.

Two specific campaigns illustrate how this has been done.

The first, the "Face the Facts" campaign, was the biggest that SHELTER has run; its aim was to clarify who the homeless were, how many were homeless, and to project housing before the nation at a time of high political tension–just before the three Party Political Conferences in 1969. The second was a counter-propaganda campaign, aimed at shattering any illusions people might have that the housing problem would be solved because a housing surplus was imminent.

Face the Facts

In March, 1969, Terence Bendixson of "The Guardian" bumped into Richard Crossman, Secretary of State for Health and Social Security, and the result of their conversation was a story in the "The Guardian" on March 15:

> **"A study of the causes of homelessness has been commissioned by Mr. Richard Crossman, Secretary for Social Services, after claims by Mr. Des Wilson, of SHELTER, that the problem is growing."**

Later, on April 29, his Junior Minister, David Ennals, announced the survey, but made his now-famous "I am speaking of truly homeless people" comment.

At this time, the Ministry were talking about "an urgent survey", the results to be released in the autumn. We were determined that the Ministry survey, based on a narrow definition, should not be allowed to pull the wool over people's eyes about the real nature of the housing emergency, and so we decided to devote our autumn campaign to hammering home our wider view of the problem, and to putting the heat into housing just before the party conferences.

The title of the report "Face the Facts" summed up its message.

A special advertising campaign was devised, based on our cynicism about the official definition.

The aim of the campaign, the public were told, was to get a re-definition of the homeless. Actually, this was an unlikely possibility, but by focusing attention on this demand, we were able to achieve the maximum publicity for the main point we wanted to make—that there were far more homeless, living in a much greater variety of appalling conditions, than was officially acknowledged.

A press conference was called, and the publicity achieved was massive—reports on all the television news programmes, and on regional programmes, and an interview on 24 Hours; and even more newspaper publicity, with many leading articles supporting SHELTER's call for a redefinition of the homeless.

London's "Evening Standard" wrote:

> **"SHELTER's revelation of the stark details have already done much to sting and activate the public conscience. Those who today live piled on top of one another, 10 families to a house, four to a bed, in the company of rats and cockroaches, will eventually have much to thank this organisation for."**

The "Northern Echo" described the report as:

> **"A sharp rebuke to statistical juggling."**

The "Bolton Evening News" said:

> **"It is to be hoped that SHELTER's report will put some effective pressure where it is most needed. The right to decent living conditions should be accepted**

as inalienable to any civilized nation."

"The Sun" said:

"It is always possible to dispute numbers. But SHELTER's evidence in detail is overwhelming and horrifying . . . as SHELTER complained, the facts have been swept under the carpet for years by all Governments. Hidden by official figures which define homelessness in the narrowest way. Figures which have afterwards to be defended even by compassionate Ministers. What SHELTER rightly asks is that the magnitude of human need should be openly admitted and that there should be no slackening in the effort to end slum conditions. What has been done in recent years to provide more houses is creditable. But let's not beat about the bush. What remains to be done is colossal."

The "Sunday Telegraph" leader said:

"Divided families, like those who share overcrowded accommodation with others or lack the elementary means of preserving privacy and health, can fairly be regarded as homeless. SHELTER does well to remind us of this. If there are only 18,689 homeless people in Britain, as official statistics claim, the problem is marginal, and its victims can too easily be linked with meths drinkers and layabouts as the inevitable sediment of a complex society. Raise the figure to a million, and a big social question presents itself causing all of us to think again."

Peter Walker, Shadow Minister of Housing, committed the Conservatives to re-defining the homeless, "to take in all families living in conditions unacceptable in a civilised society".

On the Sunday at a Rally in Trafalgar Square, the

Liberal Leader, Jeremy Thorpe, pledged himself to call on the Liberal Party to re-define the homeless.

There now followed a week of follow-up publicity and rallies. On the Monday night I was in Newcastle, appearing twice on television, and on the radio, and speaking at a public meeting. The following night at the Liberal Party Assembly, ending up on the Thursday night in Liverpool.

Two of the Liberal M.P.s, Eric Lubbock and Wallace Lawler, spoke at the SHELTER Meeting at the Liberal Party Conference, and Lubbock went on to wave a copy of the SHELTER report in front of the television cameras in a speech from the platform, and describe it as a condemnation of the priorities of our society.

Jeremy Thorpe, in his closing speech, drew his heaviest applause when he said:

> **"The worst social evil in this country is bad housing. The SHELTER report "Face the Facts" should be compulsory reading for every M.P. and every councillor in the country."**

At the close of the I.T.V. coverage of the Conference, experienced commentator and editor of the Economist, Alistair Burnett, commented on the impact of the SHELTER campaign on the Conference. It had been, he said, almost unprecedented.

From Crossman and Greenwood came no comment, but their four junior Ministers, David Ennals and Kenneth Robinson, James McColl and Lord Kennet, launched a co-ordinated counter-attack, in speeches up and down the country.

But there was standing room only at the SHELTER meeting at the Labour Party Conference the following week, chaired by Ben Whitaker, M.P., and addressed by Bruce Douglas-Mann, Frank Allaun, M.P., and myself.

When David Ennals rose to challenge the SHELTER

position, he found his remarks greeted with complete silence.

Indeed, the junior Ministers were in effect repudiated by their Prime Minister the following day. Harold Wilson had obviously been considerably impressed by the SHELTER campaign, for he took the unprecendented step of referring to SHELTER four times in his major speech to the Conference.

He began:

> **"First among the priorities of the'70s is to get rid of the scandal of bad housing and no housing. That is why all of us here are on the same side as SHELTER. Indeed we were there first.**
>
> **"I am not going to get into an arid and cold argument about how you define homelessness.**
>
> **"The problem is those without homes; the problem is those living in slums; and it is the same problem of human misery."**

He then went on to talk of the Labour Party's achievements in housing, and the Tories' failures but returning to SHELTER said:

> **"So, on this vital problem of giving all our people decent homes, we welcome the job that so many organisations are doing. We welcome, too, the urgent and passionate pressure which organisations like SHELTER can bring to this. When it comes down to it, aren't your ideals the same as theirs?"**

For all the political nuances, the most significant thing about this speech was the way he constructively aligned himself with the SHELTER campaign, in sharp contrast to the negative response of his junior Ministers. One had the feeling that Wilson was sensitive not only to the probability that housing would dominate the next General Election, but also to the popularity and strength of the SHELTER movement.

So to the Conservative Party Conference, where Reginald Maudling made posititive reference to SHELTER in his platform speech on housing, and where an amendment was carried to the housing resolution calling for special attention to the needs of the homeless, in the light of the SHELTER report.

There can be little question that both of the objectives of the "Face the Facts" campaign had been achieved: housing had not only been pushed into the forefront of public attention, but once again had become the political issue of the day. Further, from the tremendous response to SHELTER'S money raising activities towards the end of the year, it was possible to detect a much greater understanding of who the homeless were, and of their vulnerability.

The Housing Surplus

In chapter two I have explained the irrelevance of the housing surplus to Britain's housing problem.

The whole question of the housing surplus first arose in 1967 when the Minister of Housing, Anthony Greenwood, speaking in Eastbourne, referred to it. To be fair to him, he put it in perspective, saying:

> **"I have seen it said recently that the demand for housing will fall sharply in the 1970s. I am absolutely convinced that this is wrong. We know that over 100,000 houses a year will be needed simply to keep pace with the growth in households. More, we know now that we have between two and three million slums and potentially unfit houses. This indicates our major housing problem in the 1970s."**

Nevertheless, abbreviated press reports of his speech led to signs of complacency, and so SHELTER decided to make the destruction of the myth a major objective.

I wrote to Anthony Greenwood at that time to say that I thought incomplete reports of his speeches had given a misleading impression that the housing problem had practically been solved and asking him to make clear this was not so. My letter concluded:

> **"People throughout Britain must be helped to see that because the housing situation, is improving in their own districts and towns, this does not mean that millions of people in Britain are not still living in appalling squalor and will be for years. "In order that the misleading publicity be properly balanced with the real facts, I believe that you should in forthcoming publicity shift emphasis from the tremendously encouraging achievement to the huge and heart-rending problem of the homeless and the hidden homeless that still remains a major responsibility of the nation as a whole and each individual within it."**

Greenwood replied saying that he "entirely agreed" that we were not within sight of the end of the housing need. The nature of housing need and housing demand would tend to change, with less emphasis on absolute shortage–much more on rising standards, both in replacing unfit houses and in the improvement and repair of older houses which were not unfit but suffering from neglect or obsolescence. We would become more concerned with the variety of local housing needs in a number of areas.

On Thursday night, February 6, 1969 under attack from the Conservatives in the House of Commons, the Minister of Planning and Land, Kenneth Robinson, predicted a surplus of one million houses by 1973. Although he qualified this by admitting there would still be a problem of slums, and regional scarcities, he used the "housing surplus" as the main plank in his defence of the Labour administration's record, and said that a buyers' market was on the way.

"The Guardian", whose reporting of the House of Commons is particularly accurate, carried the headline on Friday, February 7: "Cathy may come home to housing surplus in 1973."

This seemed to me the height of irresponsibility for, as I've said before, whether the figure is accurate or not, it offers little hope for the people who are homeless now and will still be homeless in 1973, and was an irrelevant figure in the context of the problem. I decided to reverse the trend of the publicity and issue a press release first thing on the Friday morning condemning Robinson in the hardest possible terms.

My attack was sufficiently scathing to make "The World at One" and headlines in the evening newspapers.

The London Evening News reported:

> **"SHELTER CHIEF SLAMS COMMONS HOUSING CLAIM.**
>
> **"Mr. Kenneth Robinson's claim in the Commons yesterday that there would be a surplus of a million houses by 1973 was described by the Director of SHELTER today as 'either a cruel joke, and unscrupulous deception, or an indication of Mr. Robinson's abysmal ignorance of the realities of the housing problem.'**
>
> **"Commenting on the claim by the Minister of Planning and Land that the sellers' market would be finished, Mr. Des Wilson said there was 'a colossal difference between ending the theoretical shortage of houses and ending the real housing problem. It is not enough to have an equal number of units of accommodation to familes', he said: 'They must be in the right place at the right price, of the right standard, and of the right size. There is no chance of us meeting any of these conditions by 1973 or even 1983.' "**

"The Guardian" agreed to publish a special article by myself in the form of a letter to Cathy, explaining to her "you are the victim of a piece of political deception". That newspaper also ran a leader describing "this kind of calculation" as "an exercise in inexcusable complacency".

It said:

> **"This is an argument that the Ministry statisticians have been trotting out with great persistence in the past eighteen months or so. Why? Perhaps to justify a reduction in the housing programme that the Labour Government has been making in disregard of quite explicit election pledges. Perhaps because there has long been a desiccated gaggle of economists theorising to the effect that too large a part of the nation's resources has been going into housing. Perhaps because the party dog fight has always invited conjuring tricks with the housing figures.**
>
> **"But why should a Labour Government try to pretend that the housing situation is better than it is? It would make more sense to acknowledge the real facts which, in summary, are these. A decent home is a primary necessity for a good life, for adults and for children. Bad housing is the worst of social injustices. Several million families are living in thoroughly unsatisfactory conditions, often at excessively high rents. Even if in a few years time there are in total more dwellings than households, they will not all be in the right places, or of the right kind, or at prices ordinary people can afford to rent or buy. The deterioration of old dwellings is likely to outpace their replacement or renovation at the present rate of progress.**
>
> **"We do not know the true demand for new dwellings because there is no reliable estimate of the number of families sharing accommodation who would want to**

> **move to something better if they had the chance or could afford it (the longer and longer waiting lists for council houses and flats suggests that it must be large). True demand for decent housing is marred by high rents and high mortgage rates which discourage many families from even looking for a better home. Compared with other European countries, we are putting too small a share of our national resources into housing. Even with a much more ambitious housing programme, the revolution of rising expectations will run away from us, and the next generation will demand better standards than their parents were prepared to put up with. And that will be true in 1999, never mind 1973."**

On the Friday afternoon "24 Hours" decided to stage a debate between Robinson and myself. An invitation was "tentatively" issued to me at 4 p.m. and accepted. At 5.30 p.m. the researcher concerned rang to say it was "definitely" confirmed, and made arrangements for me to be picked up at my home at 9 p.m. I left to go home, and about 7 p.m., the researcher, who had carried out all the negotiations, rang to say that the Minister had refused to appear with me and that the invitation must be "regretfully withdrawn". I asked whether Robinson was not appearing then, but he explained that the Minister was anxious to appear, but that he would not agree to appear with me. Robinson then went on "24 Hours" and claimed that I had attacked him without knowledge of what he had said in the House.

I saw no reason why he should be allowed to get away with this, and so issued, through the Press Association, the facts about the "24 Hours" programme.

The result was that the story made the front pages of every national newspaper the next day. Robinson had, by refusing to debate with me, made certain that the maximum attention would be drawn to my answer to his claims in the House of Commons. From then on throughout 1969 I continued to hammer away at the housing surplus, whenever it arose.

Finally, the top politicians at the Ministry decided that one particular criticism in "The Guardian" had to be answered, and so poor Frank Judd, the M.P. for Portsmouth, who was Greenwood's p.p.s., was given a letter to send. Judd tried to palm it off on at least one other M.P., and having failed, duly posted it.

In it he claimed that Robinson had been misquoted, and his comments taken out of context.

He also claimed the figures were accurate.

I replied:

> **"SHELTER does not bother to argue with the authorities about the probability of a crude housing surplus in the 1970s, or the accuracy of their statistics, for they are irrelevant to the housing problem. The increasingly bitter row between not only SHELTER, but all other people in the front line of the fight for the homeless, and the authorities, is over the context in which the statistics about a potential housing surplus are used, and the effect of their constant repetition by the Minister and his colleagues.**
>
> **"For all their qualifications about the importance of the statistics, Ministry spokesmen continued to use them in the context of a defence of the Government's recent housing record.**
>
> **"It is they who dragged the statistics in whenever the housing problem is mentioned. If they, too, believe that the surplus is irrelevant to the housing problem, why don't they stop referring to it?**
>
> **"Whether they like it or not, they are giving the impression that the problem is nearly solved. Their apparent complacency is leading to a running down**

> **of the housing programme and a lack of confidence in the housing industry.**
> **"Experienced politicians should know it is not what you say that counts, but what people hear. By using these statistics in the context of the housing problem, they automatically lead people to connect the two. Their qualifications are irrelevant, for qualifications, as they know only too well, never get much publicity."**

I've given considerable emphasis to the "housing surplus" in this book, both in order to drive another nail into its coffin, and also because the success of this campaign shows again the importance of single-minded obstinacy in pressure activity, and also the important role that the well-informed volunteer can play in moulding public opinion, by challenging propaganda where that propaganda is either unfair or potentially dangerous.

SHELTER's Comment . . ."

One of the ways that a well-informed pressure group can be highly effective is by being first to comment on its subject whenever it becomes topical.

I put high priority on the creation within SHELTER of what I called our "propaganda unit". This consisted of an efficient press office, that was capable of writing, duplicating, and distributing press releases round Fleet Street in just over an hour, but could write a press release and dictate it to the Press Association in a matter of minutes if required; a full time photographer, with his own dark room, who could take pictures, develop them, and distribute them quickly; and a designer, who could get a leaflet produced in 24 hours if an emergency arose.

In addition, the research and information office was responsible for getting the early editions of the evening papers, also all the morning newspapers, reading them carefully, and distributing to the relevant people any items that might require comment.

Also, we established contacts in the House of Commons with people who kept us informed of what parliamentary questions were being tabled to the Minister of Housing, and anything else that might arise in the House.

This meant that should a speech be made in the morning, SHELTER could have its comments in the late editions of the evening newspapers.

For instance, when Enoch Powell made a speech one morning criticising the existence of council houses, we were able to pick it up in the first edition of the Evening Standard, and have our own comments extensively reported in the last editions. Our comments carried over onto radio broadcasts and into the morning newspapers.

This is one of the great values of a professional pressure group, acting on behalf of the poor. With the expertise at hand, SHELTER has been able to act as a voice for the homeless on issues such as this.

Legislation

A charity is prohibited from calling for specific legislation, but it can nevertheless play a major role in bringing it about.

SHELTER has, for instance, played a major part in getting the Francis Committee set up, to look into the workings of the Rent Act.

After the Rent Act was passed in 1965, and consolidated in the 1968 Rent Act, many people remained extremely concerned about its workings.

An so in 1968 SHELTER decided to devote its autumn campaign to an investigation of the workings of the Rent Act, particularly in relation to eviction and harassment. A report was published called "Notice to Quit" and was also massively publicised.

The report pinpointed 13 areas of insecurity that still

remained, and cited many case histories.

The implications of this research were hammered home at meetings at the Party Conferences, and SHELTER decided to back them up by creating pressure for action.

As SHELTER could not call for specific legislation or legislative change, it had set the scene for campaigns by other people, both by producing vital evidence and by increasing public knowledge, about the inadequacies of the Rent Act.

Now SHELTER went further, by setting up a Rent Act Conference in June, 1969, which brought together everybody concerned about this problem in a hotel in London. A full transcript of the Conference, together with the recommendations of a study group set up by the Conference, was sent to the Minister.

As the study group was set up by the Conference, and only the Conference was sponsored by SHELTER, it was possible to claim that the changes of legislation demanded were being sought by the study group, and not by SHELTER itself.

This was followed up by a strong campaign, led by Bruce Douglas-Mann, a member of the study group, at the Labour Party Conference. As well as moving a resolution at the Conference, Bruce spoke at the SHELTER meeting.

The end result was the setting up of the Francis Committee, and the SHELTER Conference transcript and the study group's notes were the first items of evidence received.

Assessing Pressure

It is not an easy task to assess effectively the results of pressure activities.

The difference between the SHELTER operation and, for example, the activities of the Stop the Seventy Tour, is that the latter objective was easily defined and could be achieved by one straightforward decision. The Stop the

Seventy Tour Committee were outstandingly effective, and their campaign is undoubtedly an inspiration to all who are campaigning for radical causes. But it is not easy to compare it with the necessarily sustained efforts by pressure groups in more complicated fields.

The pressure activities of SHELTER are not easily assessed, for two reasons:

Firstly, they have been up until now largely concerned with heightening public interest, and one of the effects of this is to introduce new groups into the field, who in turn share the credit for the concern aroused.

Secondly, pioneering organisations are often not able, themselves, to convert their activities into national policy, and have to encourage the authorities to take up their ideas, at the expense of obtaining the credit for them when they become policy. Indeed, it is not in the interests of "the system" for the authorities to admit that they have given way to pressure. Thus, to be effective, the pressure group must often fade quietly away when its objectives are achieved, and certainly the authorities will rarely concede that they have been influenced, partly because they don't regard it in their interests to encourage other pressure groups to form.

In one sense I believe that the SHELTER pressure activities have been remarkably effective. In another they have failed.

For instance, SHELTER has not succeeded in getting the worthwhile increases in private and public expenditure on housing that it has sought.

Yet it has projected housing into the forefront of public attention, and kept it there.

The easiest conclusion to draw from this is that responsible pressure activity is just not going to be effective in getting greater priority for housing, but this perhaps overlooks the possibility that SHELTER itself has put too much emphasis on fresh expenditure, and not enough on pressing for more effective use of existing expenditure.

I have already explained why it was decided that our pressure activities should emphasise the need for even greater expenditure, and I think this decision was the only practical one at the time.

However, it now appears as though the kind of reappraisal of housing subsidies that is urged in Chapter 5 of this book may come about. If it does, and if some of the other policies advocated in that Chapter are linked to it, we might be able to assess more realistically where fresh money is needed, and the pressure to get that money might be more effective.

Undoubtedly politicians of both major parties have been able to argue against increasing the proportion of the G.N.P. spent on housing on the grounds that "we're not making the best use of existing money." This argument would be less effective if we were making the best use of that money and it was still insufficient.

It seems to me that whichever policy SHELTER had adopted in its first two or three years might have been wrong: the one it chose, to concentrate on greater expenditure, has not up until now achieved much, but had SHELTER begun immediately to voice its opinion on housing policies, it would not have done so with the authority and the experience that it now has, and as a result might not have gained the influence that it can now bring to bear.

What, then, has been gained from arousing public opinion?

Firstly, the involvement of far more people in a voluntary capacity, both through SHELTER, and many other types of housing groups.

Secondly, the injection of political heat into housing. *This might not have boosted the housing programme but may have avoided even worse results than were achieved.*

Thirdly, a more enlightened public about the complexities of the housing problem should make the introduction of radical solutions more acceptable. Paradoxically, although this aroused public opinion has been created largely in protest at the mediocre achievements of politicians in the past, it also offers them their greatest opportunities for the future. Politicians who really *want* to get results know how to use public opinion to that end.

Leaving aside the main aim–an increase in expenditure–I believe that SHELTER has had much more influence on housing policy than has been recognised, or will be conceded.

The transition by national and local government to a balanced programme of new building and rehabilitation has been made a lot easier because of the experience in this field of the voluntary housing movement, and because of the wider public acceptance of the importance of rehabilitation that owes much to SHELTER's educational activity.

SHELTER and the big housing associations made rehabilitation not only acceptable, but exciting, and in selling the concept of neighbourhood rehabilitation because it believed it to be the *right* concept, SHELTER was, in fact, doing much to make Government action, through the 1969 Housing Act, more potentially effective.

At the time of this book going to print Lambeth became the first Council to open up a housing advisory centre, and received a lot of publicity for it. At the same time, it was announced that the Institute of Housing Managers was to devote one of its main sessions at its 1970 Conference to the subject of housing aid and advice.

Who devised housing aid and advice, and sold it to the authorities–Eamonn Casey, as Director of Catholic Housing Aid Society and Chairman of SHELTER.

Who set up the first major experiment in housing aid and advice?–SHELTER, with its SHAC in London.

When it became clear that the 1969 Housing Act was

going to make possible not just neighbourhood rehabilitation, but rehabilitation with the full participation of people in the area, who was it that set up the first comprehensive scheme, involving a coalition of local authority, and people in the area? SHELTER, with its Liverpool SNAP.

Experiment is by no means the most spectacular form of pressure activity. No violence, no demonstrators, no policemen, and often no praise when the results are achieved.

It's hard work, and it's quiet work, and it often takes a long time. It took Eamonn Casey nearly ten years to see housing aid and advice finally accepted as being essential to the application of housing policy.

It's taken the more articulate spokesmen for rehabilitation twenty years to get an Act that has the potential of the 1969 Housing Act.

But, even then, they only achieved this because they proved their point, over a period of time, ironing out the faults themselves, and handing to the authorities a tried and tested product with a positive application.

These achievements are not SHELTER's alone. They are the achievements of the voluntary housing movement, and its experience over many years, coupled with the salesmanship and influence of SHELTER at the crucial stage.

As the details about the SHELTER rescue operation in Chapter 9, and the details of our pressure activity in this Chapter, must have made clear, the projection of the SHELTER campaign, with its sense of urgency, has not been as easy as it would appear. For the SHELTER operation itself is a highly complicated one, involving the integration of a variety of different activities, but I believe as the years go by its pressure achievements will begin to multiply at what could become a startling rate, and it could become a classic argument for reforming our society by linking experiment and example with the enthusiasm and idealism that, whilst crucially important, are in themselves no answer to a complicated problem.

Pressure Tomorrow

During 1970 the SHELTER team has discussed both the need to make SHELTER itself a more democratic movement, and from this additional strength to be more effective as a co-ordinator of local pressure activity.

Helene Middleweek, only the second girl to become President of the Cambridge Union, was appointed our first Pressure Co-ordinator. Her brief was to take up any local housing issues drawn to our attention, research them, and then recommend to SHELTER how it might best bring its influence to bear.

Much of her activity in 1970 is bound to be experimental, for SHELTER still has a lot to learn about pressure at local level.

But the aim is to make available to our local Groups throughout the country an expertise and experience that will enable them to get more humane policies and attitudes towards the homeless in their own area, and to be effectively militant in local housing affairs.

SHELTER's aim at the time of writing is to create a situation where it is carrying out a well-informed and well-tested campaign for more realistic national policies, and a highly-sensitive campaign for more humane attitudes in the Town Hall.

It will add to this the provision of information and advice and, I hope, a degree of co-ordination to all of the other housing groups springing up.

This Chapter began with Eleanor Roosevelt's famous words about human rights—"Where after all do human rights begin? In small places, close to home."

It is out in the community that SHELTER's influence may be most needed. If it is to succeed, it will not do it with a national reputation and a national team alone. If housing priorities, and human in financial terms, are to be achieved, every man and woman who cares about human rights and equality of opportunity must stand up and be counted.

Every member of the public has the right to contribute to the correspondence columns of local newspapers. Everyone has a member of parliament to whom he can write or talk. Everyone has a local councillor through whom to channel requests for action. Everyone has local political parties, and local organisations, through which they can campaign.

The opportunities are there in abundance for every one of us to play our part.

POSTSCRIPT

> **"Life is tragic simply because the earth turns and the sun inescerably rises and sets, and one day, for each of us the sun will go down for the last time. Perhaps the whole root of our trouble, the human trouble, is that we will sacrifice all of the beauty of our lives, will imprison ourselves in totems, taboos, crosses, blood sacrifices, steeples, mosques, races, armies, flags, nations, in order to deny the fact of death, which is the only fact we have. It seems to me that one ought to rejoice in the fact of death–ought to side indeed to *earn* one's death by confronting with passion the conundrum of life. One is responsible to life."**
>
> *James Baldwin*

A MESSAGE OF HOPE

Participants rarely make patient spectators, and activists are not the most objective of commentators.

I am too near in terms of my contribution, and the events too near in time, for me to be able to put the work of SHELTER in real perspective.

There is, though, one claim I can make. I've been constructive.

Neither the wastelands of our urban slums, nor the unkindled idealism of our young people, should be playgrounds for the political opportunist or the well-intentioned but unrealistic demagogue.

Some of the activities that take place in the name of the poor border on exploitation of their need. Some of their advocates, though well-intentioned, can be disastrous for their cause.

One thinks of the Squatters at 144 Piccadilly who, when interviewed on radio and television, claimed to be highlighting the problems of the homeless. This no doubt added a little respectability to their activities. I leave my reader to judge what good it did the homeless!

The homeless will disappear when the housing problem is solved, and it will not be solved by puritanical fervour, or aggression that is not linked to specific and realistic targets.

Neither I nor my friends in s,SHELTER ever claimed a sole perogative to care, nor that we were the only people in Britain most likely to come up with an answer to the housing problem. But what we've at all times sought to do is to present *a balanced case with urgency*–and this is more difficult than it sounds.

Many worthwhile people have been putting forward sound and valuable policies for solving the housing problem for a long time. Many others have projected the needs of the homeless with great urgency. The difficult role that SHELTER undertook was to combine the two. To thump home the needs of the homeless with all the power we could muster. And then to push for better programmes and greater financial priority on the basis of well-informed argument and rapidly-accumulated experience.

I think we've shown that idealism and realism can go together, and it is only when they are linked that idealism really flourishes.

There is no greater tragedy than to see the idealism of young people crushed by the frustration of wasted effort.

Even worse is to see them pursue their idealism with an inconsistency that is bound to fail.

Speaking at a school prize-giving in London in 1968, I argued the case for the SHELTER approach to protest as follows:

> **"You cannot oppose violence with violence. You cannot destroy prejudice by feeding it. You cannot expect people to accept your ideals when your own actions do not reflect them. The inevitable result of violent protest will be a wave of prejudice against the young, and a step by society backwards into a defensive position instead of forwards to change. I would urge you to choose a constructive form of protest. Show your refusal to accept society's priorities by directly taking on the responsibilities that it abdicates. The way to alter the system is to outclass it on its own terms. Thus you fight the apathy about, say, the housing problem, not in Whitehall, but in your own community. Seek to change attitudes by fighting in the places where our own society is vulnerable and where its values are seen to be wrong–fight in the slums, not in Grosvenor Square. Create a platform of achievement that earns you the right to speak out, and equips you with the knowledge and experience to make your voice heard and respected.**
>
> **"And most important, this achievement will feed your idealism and equip you for the ultimate responsibility that you, as the next ruling generation, must assume.**
>
> **"The tragedy of those who hit out at everything and miss the lot, is that they end up disillusioned and their energy, enthusiasm, idealism and imagination is lost. Through active participation in the community, yours can flourish."**

Occasionally I find myself confronted with revolutionaries, often in staged debates on radio or television. Somehow the aim has been to make myself as a reformer seem old-fashioned, and the revolutionary ultra-modern. For myself, I've always regarded the revolutionary as out-of-date, or at least misplaced, in the sense we do not live in a revolutionary situation, or even a potentially revolutionary situation.

We are living in a society where the majority are catered for, both by a wide range of employment opportunities, and by a fairly comprehensive welfare state. The problems of the minority are partly problems of isolation, as well as of inflexibility of "the system" that has been set up to serve the majority.

This situation calls for effective communicators and reformers, not for revolutionaries to whom the poor and the homeless are often merely weapons in their armoury.

It is extraordinary, though, how much opportunity there is for imaginative involvement within reformist movements.

One of the most exciting aspects of the Liverpool SNAP scheme is that it opens up the opportunity for an area to draw on its own suppressed idealism and imagination and bring about change that can never be legislated for alone.

Provided one accepts the principle that one should build on the existing legislative and organisational structure of a society, and change it, but not set out to destroy it totally, the opportunities for imaginative and ruthlessly-determined participation are colossal.

It has been heartbreaking to see the concept of participation taken up by the liberals in our society, discussed at interminable length, unenthusiastically legislated for, and then allowed to fade away, when in fact it offers our society so much.

Perhaps the greatest hope for our cities lies in maximum participation of the people in their improvement, and indeed in a situation where people potter about in their towns and cities in the way that they have, up to now, pottered about in their gardens.

For myself, I find it hard to be totally sympathetic to the man who complains endlessly about the politicians but who can point to no constructive contribution that he makes to his street, village, town, or city, let alone his country, other than grudgingly paying rates and taxes.

Narrow lives lead to narrow minds. Intolerance and selfishness in our society exists least among those who share their problems and recognise that their health and well-being ultimately depends on the health and well-being of society as a whole.

I think the message of SHELTER is one of *hope*. In the compassion and generosity of all the people who have contributed so much of their own money we see *hope* of a willingness to share. In the thousands of families being rescued can be found *hope* for others as yet unreached. In the experiments in housing aid and advice can be found *hope* of more humane and sensitive treatment of the poor. In the neighbourhood action project lies *hope* for the revitalisation of whole communities, people, environment, and housing. In the achievement and aspirations of the many, many young people involved in SHELTER can be found real *hope* of a better society tomorrow. In the success of SHELTER and the voluntary housing movement in influencing housing policy, and in the success of SHELTER in balancing pressure activity with rescue, can be found *hope* that the volunteer can be justifiably influential in our local and national affairs.

In SHELTER's popularity in the face of the more superficially exciting activities of the revolutionary lies *hope* for a victory for reason and tolerance over society's potential for prejudice and violence.

Undoubtedly there is a great deal to be done. But, as Dr. Johnson said, "When there is no hope, there can be no endeavour."

SHELTER in its revelations about the poor and the homeless and in its record of achievements so far is, above all, encouragement to greater endeavour.

"Hope ever urges on, and tells us tomorrow will be better."